ASTROLOGY AND YOU

ASTROLOGY AND YOU

Gopesh Kumar Ojha
Ashutosh Ojha

MOTILAL BANARSIDASS PUBLISHERS
PRIVATE LIMITED ● DELHI

Reprint: 2008
First Edition: Delhi, 2002
(Earlier published in 1973 under the title *Astrology for All*)

ISBN : 978-81-208-1930-6 (Cloth)
ISBN : 978-81-208-1918-4 (Paper)

MOTILAL BANARSIDASS

41 U.A. Bungalow Road, Jawahar Nagar, Delhi 110 007
8 Mahalaxmi Chamber, 22 Bhulabhai Desai Road, Mumbai 400 026
203 Royapettah High Road, Mylapore, Chennai 600 004
236, 9th Main III Block, Jayanagar, Bangalore 560 011
Sanas Plaza, 1302 Baji Rao Road, Pune 411 002
8 Camac Street, Kolkata 700 017
Ashok Rajpath, Patna 800 004
Chowk, Varanasi 221 001

PRINTED IN INDIA
BY JAINENDRA PRAKASH JAIN AT SHRI JAINENDRA PRESS,
A-45, NARAINA, PHASE-I, NEW DELHI 110 028
AND PUBLISHED BY NARENDRA PRAKASH JAIN FOR
MOTILAL BANARSIDASS PUBLISHERS PRIVATE LIMITED,
BUNGALOW ROAD, DELHI 110 007

PREFACE

मंगलाचरण

आपदामपहन्तारं दातारं सर्वसम्पदाम्।
लोकाभिरामं श्रीरामं भूयो भूयो नमाम्यहम्॥

The Destroyer of all misfortunes, the Giver of all affluence,
the Bestower of all happiness, I bow again and again to
Shri Rama.

When we wrote the present book we had in mind those of
you who are acquainted with the term Astrology or Jyotish,
but did not understand how to use it for their daily needs.
They keep going on to an astrologer every time an important
event has occurred or decision has to be made. With this
statement we do not want to undermine the importance of
an astrologer—an expert in his profession has no parallel.
However, if someone in the family has headaches we give
him a pain-killer *viz.,* anacin, aspro etc., or for small and
minor injuries apply a balm and a small bandage at home.
We do not rush to a doctor or call an ambulance all the time.

To come back to the present book we assure that reading
this will equip you in the first instance with substantial
knowledge so that you are able to ask better questions and
understand Astrology properly.

It is possible that in the beginning the mathematical part
may appear to be tiring to a few. However for all that, we
have now softwares which do all the necessary calculations
accurate and fast.

When the calculation part is done you need to understand
the basic meanings of planets and houses in order to decipher
correctly. If you do not know anything than the chart will
look like 'Talisman'.

If we may be bold enough and suggest to the courageous and strong minded readers who value truth to spend a few weeks with this work (and a few weeks are necessary). Once you have the grasp of the basic subject-matter, you can go ahead and examine your own horoscope as well as the horoscopes of people around you. With experience and knowledge so gained one can arm oneself to get a warning of the coming events and 'Forewarned is Forearmed'.

The local saying is that a new Astrologer and an old (experienced) Vaidya are better. The new Astrologer is better because he is not lost into the pros and cons of the principles of astrology and sticks to the basics.

Who is a good astrologer? The answer is one who is pleasant in appearance; has consideration for others, is religious and God-fearing, has respect for the ethics of life, has full knowledge of the subject-matter, is not cunning and does not have his own wheel to grind. Such a person is the right astrologer.

Astrology is not for people who are fearful, who can not face the truth and go into tempers and/or depression when faced with the coming shadows cast by malefics *viz.*, Rahu, Ketu, Saturn and Mars. They keep on brooding making life miserable not only for themselves but for people all around them. They do not understand that when we drive a car and the road signs tell us that there are bumps and dangerous curves ahead, we become careful and drive cautiously. We do not abandon the car and keep brooding.

We have life so we will have problems, we have mind so we will have worries, we have intellect so we will have negative thoughts. This is life and it moves in cycles.

Astrology or Jyotish illuminates what is in store for us. It tells when to take action and when to lie low. We should use this knowledge of the 'Vedas' for improving our life. Directing the energies into the proper channels when the times are favourable, will ensure easy success *i.e.*, success with less efforts.

We now state certain matters not mentioned in books but these may help us to analyse certain problems in life:

There are times when the body temperature is one degree above normal in general. The reason is that when we pass through the periods, Major or Minor, of Mars, it increases the temperature in the system. In the same manner during the periods of Moon, one feels comparatively colder.

Similarly, in life chronic fatigue comes and it defying all logic lasts for a few weeks to almost thirty-eight months. The reason in this case is that during the Minor period of Venus in the Major period of Saturn and vice versa, fatigue comes. There are exceptions and that is, if Venus and Saturn are placed in one House or have a Sambandh, then they confer a very auspicious time in the major period of one and the minor period of the other. By taking vitamins and calcium, the health is improved.

One's temperament and physical appearance is transformed as one takes the hue and lustre of a planet whose mahadasha and antardashas one is passing through. A good or evil transit also affects the entire personality. The tolerance and anger manifests, the skin colour undergoes changes, the desires increase or subsides for various activities.

The timing of events is very important. Just as a seed when planted at the right season and right time, turns into a grand tree with flowers and fruits, so the selection of an auspicious time for marriage, opening up of new office, expansion in business, signing of an agreement or contract is very much needed for ensuring success.

Some of us cannot read books in Sanskrit so this book, *Astrology and You* in English language will be a boon for you. It enunciates the principles of Astrology as laid down by Mahrishi Parashar, Mantreshwar, Kali Das and other Sages.

A question is sometimes raised that many a times exalted planets in various charts do not show good results. Look at the Horoscope of Shri Rama:

Horoscope

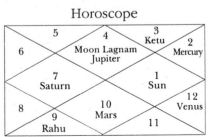

With so many exalted planets what did he get out of Life? Exalted Mars in the 7th House (wife) made him fight to get wedded; to fight and get her back from Ravana; to discard and abandon her even after she was made to prove her purity through Agni Pariksha and then to lose her in the end.

Exalted Saturn made him wander in forest due to a mother for 14 years. Exalted Sun (His Vanaprastha) was the cause of his father's death. His Moon in Cancer and exalted Jupiter could not protect him from the venom of Saturn from the fourth and the blast of Mars from the seventh house---And all of them exalted.

His exalted Venus and strong Moon in the chart did give a beautiful wife endowed with the qualities most desirable in a woman but she was also one of the cause of his problems. So Exalted Planets are they good?

Although the question raised above is a very debatable one yet the answer is that it is nice to have exalted planets but debilitated planets should not be condemned.

No planet is good or bad. All of them have three types of tendencies *viz.*, of the earthly level or of the rajsik level or of spiritual level:

Venus

a. Love for women, wine, luxurious life, desires in abundance.
b. Artists, poets, musicians, actors and fame in these lines.
c. Divine love, Bhakti marg (like Shri Chaitanya, Sh. Hari Das, Sh. Ramakrishna adopted).

Jupiter

a. Gluttons, sumptuous food eaters, always laughing and cracking jokes which are not of high taste. Blood disorders or chronic headaches.
b. Bankers, financial managers, persons doing charitable work expecting to receive recognition, Conjugal Bliss and longevity for husband in case of a woman. No happiness from son/sons.

c. A sanyasi, a recluse, still wealth follows him, famous if a king.

Mercury

a. Success in journalism, writing money from properties; some good friends. At times an egoist; cunning, unfaithful and sharp.
b. Fame in acting, recognition and honour, subtle sense of humour, good lawyers, beautiful hand-writing, famous surgeons.
c. Worshippers of lord Vishnu and Krishna. Learned Sanyasis and great Astrologers (soothsayers).

Sun

a. Strong Soul, arrogance and pride of being from a high family.
b. Helping attitudes towards others; Love for the family, father in particular; An aristocratic look but not arrogant.
c. Spiritual, Kings and Commanders who are wise and renounce in the end. Worshipper of Sun. Whatever they say comes true. There is a glow on their face.

Mars

a. Courage, accident prone, at times bullies, fondness for sports, can be quarrelsome.
b. Well behaved, polite, army commanders, doctors of medicine, physically fit and strong and honourable, problems in married life.
c. Many brothers; problems on account of brothers, success, powerful kings, fame, expert in warfare.

Saturn

a. Benefit from Lands (agricultural) and ancestral property, antiques, old people, oil etc.

b. Renunciation in young age (Like Adi Shankara), Anandmayi Ma. Disenchantment with life as in the case of Prabhupada. All of them had Exalted Saturn.

c. Recluse. Poverty. True Sanyasi due to disenchantment with 'Maya'.

Moon

a. Popularity with the masses. Oversensitive by nature. Fat in appearance.

b. Wealth and success. Unhappy married life. Love affair with married women or a widow (good looking).

c. Excessive talkers, high imagination, psychics, hypersensitive, psychitzopherania.

By understanding Astrology, we shall be able to avoid pitfalls. When we realize that an exalted Saturn may take away even the basic necessities of life so that one is drawn towards God.

Exalted Jupiter may make one lost to this world. The 'Bhuval Sanyasi' case. He had an exalted Jupiter in the 8th house. Poisoned by his own queen and saved by wandering Sanyasis, he moved and travelled with them for a duration of sixteen years of Jupiter Mahadasha. He had lapse of memory but all of this passed in the beginning of Saturn. His memory came back and he won his kingdom.

We have found Exalted Venus in the horoscopes of addicts but ultimately Divine Love changed it all. Realization of the Lord through Chanting and Music. (See case of Sur Das).

This is a complete book and when you read it, you become a master of the subject. We have kept it simple and methodical to suit the taste of everyone. The subject-matter has been properly dealt with. An appendix gives the precession of the equinoxes (ayanamsa) on First of January. The exact Ayanamsa can be taken from the Lahiri's or any other ephemerides for that year.

Some Astrological words as well as Sanskrit words are added in the end. Their brief meanings and pages where they occur are mentioned for ready reference.

ॐ शान्ति·
असतो मा सद्गमय
तमसो मा ज्योतिर्गमय।
मृत्योर्मामृत गमय॥

OM SHANTI
From the unreal lead me to the Real;
From darkness lead me to Light;
From death lead me to Immortality.

93, Daryaganj   —ASHUTOSH OJHA
New Delhi - 110002
aojha@vsnl.com

CONTENTS

Friendship Among Planets—Natural Friendship, Neutrality and Enmity—Temporary Relationship—Resultant Relationship—Example Worked Out—Effect of a Planet Occupying a House of Great Friend, Friend, Neutral, Enemy or Great Enemy—Benefics and Malefics—Aspects—Directions—Colours, Jewels and Metals—Sex—Ingredients of Body—Taste—Directional Strength—Planets as Significators—Combust Planets.

Planet in own Sign—Exception—The Ascendant or The Moon in the Twelve Signs—Aries, Taurus, Gemini etc.—Effect of Sun being in Different Signs—Mars Occupying a Particular Sign—Effect of Mercury in Each of the Twelve Signs—Jupiter's Location in Different Signs—Venus Occupying Aries, Taurus, Gemini etc.—Saturn's Location in the Twelve Signs—Favourable Signs for Rahu's Tenancy—Ketu.

Position of Planets and Modifying Influences—Sun, Moon, Mars, Mercury, Jupiter, Venus, Saturn, Rahu and Ketu Occupying the First House—Effect of Each of the Planets in the Second, Third, Fourth, Fifth, Sixth, Seventh, Eighth, Ninth, Tenth, Eleventh or the Twelfth House.

General Guidelines—Lord of the House and the Various Factors Which Make it Strong or Weak—Location in Sign and *Navansha*—Dispositor of the Sign and *Navansha*—House Position—Conjunction with Planets—The Aspects a Planet Receives—Combust—Hemmed in between Benefics or Malefics—Judgment of a House—Tenanted by Benefics or Malefics—Aspects on the House—Hemmed in between Planets—Tenancy of Planets on other Houses Affecting the House under Examination—Houses Counted from the Moonsign—*Karakas* for Houses—Scrutiny of *Karaka*—Judgment of the Body, Parts of the Body, Temperament, Diseases, Wealth, Poverty, Immovable Properties, Speech, Brothers and Sisters, Mother, Conveyances, Friends, Happiness, Education, Children, Gain from Betting, Enemies, Wife, Husband, Longevity, Legacy, Religiousness, Foreign Trips, Father, Career, Agriculture, Service, Independent Profession, Trade and Commerce—Good *Yogas*—Combinations for Wealth and Position Selected from Standard Sanskrit Works.

Various Systems of Planetary Periods—The Most Popular and Widely

Practised System—Table A Specifying Periods for Each of The Nine Planets—Nine Sub-divisions in Each of the Periods—Table B Specifying Order and Duration of Each Sub-period—How to Determine Ruling Period at Birth—Sub-division of the Zodiac into 27 Sectors—*Nakshatras*—Table C Giving Domain of Each *Nakshatra*—Example Worked Out—Balance of Period at Birth—Example—Sub-period in the Example Chart.

CHAPTER X : TIMING OF EVENTS ...113

Events Fructify according to Indications in the Birth Chart—General Principles to Determine Quality of Planetary Influence—House Effects According to Ownership, Tenancy and Aspect—Planet Owning Two Houses—Placement in Signs Rising Head First Etc.—Rahu And Ketu—The First Test—Planet as Significator or *Karaka* According as it is Weak or Strong—Sun, Moon, Mars, Mercury, Jupiter, Venus, Saturn, Rahu and Ketu—The Second Test According as the Lord of the House is Strong or Weak—The Lords of 1st, 2nd, 3rd, 4th, 5th, 6th, 7th, 8th, 9th, 10th, 11th and 12th House—The Third Test—A Planet Owning Good or Bad Houses—*Yoga Karaka*—*Maraka*—Key Planets for each of the Ascendants—Aries, Taurus, Gemini, Cancer, Leo, Virgo, Libra, Scorpio, Sagittarius, Capricorn, Aquarius and Pisces—Judgment of Sub-periods—General Principles Governing the Quality of Effects—Some Rough and Ready Methods for Fixing Timings—Wearing Jewels to Ward off Evil Influence of Planets.

CHAPTER XI : TRANSITS ...135

Utility of Timing Events by Transits—What is a Transit—Moonsign at Birth—Transits of Sun—Good and Evil Effects—When They are Obstructed—Favourable and Unfavourable Transits of the Moon—When Held under Check—Mars when Good or Evil by Transit—When Transit Effects are Nullified—Favourable and Unfavourable Transits of Mercury—when the Influence does not Operate—Good and Evil Transits of Jupiter, Timings when they do not Show Effect—Transits of Venus—When the Transit is Ineffectual—Transits of Saturn—Good and Evil—When the Operative Influence Does Not Fructify—Transits of Rahu and Ketu.

CHAPTER I

WHAT IS ASTROLOGY

Astrology is the science of the heavens in relation to its effects on human beings. We know, the earth is very small as compared with the Sun and goes round it completing one orbit in 365 days, 6 hours, 9 minutes and 9.7 seconds. As compared with trillions of stars, the earth is a mere speck. Many of the fixed stars are so distant from earth that it takes thousands of years for light to travel from them to us. And light travels at the rate of 1,86,000 miles per second. So the magnitude of the heavens can better be imagined than described.

Many people contest the theory that the stars and the planets can affect human beings on earth. But the practical experience of thousands of years has confirmed that the Sun, Moon etc. not only emit heat, light, magnetism, electricity and other energies known to science but other subtler forces which profoundly influence life on earth. We are aware, how, the heat of the Sun not only creates weather conditions, ripening of crops and other natural phenomena. We are also aware how changes in sun-spots affect radiowaves passing through the earth's atmosphere. Many scientists have established a correlation between the cycle of the sun-spots and periods of economic depression on our planet. The effect of the Moon on the seas causes high and low tides is too familiar a phenomenon to be elaborated. Many diseases such as asthma and epilepsy have a direct connection with the digits of the Moon. The word lunacy comes from luna which means 'the moon' and persons born at a time when the Moon is weak and severely afflicted in the heavens, suffer from derangement of the mind or lunacy. The menstrual cycle in women is distinctly the lunar cycle of twenty-eight days.

Not only Hindus, but practically all the old civilisations on earth believed in the science of astrology.

Says Sidney K. Bennett, "Astrology's scientists and students are numbered by hundreds among the world's greatest of all time. Students of this science are in very good company, for they are standing side by side with Moses, Newton, Emerson, Kepler, Harems, Plato, Ptolemy, Zoroaster, Abraham, Thales, Anacimander, Hippocrates, Bacon, Napier, Flamstead, Cardan, Placidus, Brahe, Shakespeare, Byron, Scott, Dryden, Chaucer, Goethe, Copernicus, Galileo, Regiomontanus, Paracelsus and countless other guardians of wisdom in all ages and in all lands."

Here are a few excerpts from Shakespeare referring to the influence of the stars and the planets on human affairs.

"...And by my prescience
I find my Zenith doth depend upon
A most auspicious star, whose influence
If now I court not, but omit, my fortunes
Will ever after droop..."

(*The Tempest* I-ii)

"So planet-like would I o'ersway his state
That he should be my fool and I his fate."

(*Love's Labour Lost* V-ii)

"Lo at their births good stars were opposite."

(*King Richard the Third* IV-vi)

"The heavens themselves, the planets and this centre
Observe degree, priority and place
Insisture, course, proportion, season, form
Office and custom, in all lines of order."

(*Troilus And Cressida* I-iii)

"If I do wake, some planet strike me down."
(Titus Andronicus II-iv)
"...for my mind misgives
Some consequence, yet hanging in the stars
Shall bitterly begin his fearful date."

(*Romeo and Juliet* I-iv)

"And shake the yoke of inauspicious stars
From this world wearied flesh, Eyes look your last."

(*Romeo and Juliet* V-iii)

"A soothsayer bids you beware the ides of March."[1]

(Julius Ceaser I-ii)

"When beggars die, there are no comets seen.
The heavens themselves blaze forth the death of Princes."

(Julius Ceaser II-ii)

The annals of history are replete with references to the science of astrology and how predictions made on the basis of stars have been fulfilled. With Hindus, astrology is a part of the religion itself. The *Vedas,* the *Puranas* and the epics are all full of astrological lore and perhaps in no country of the world, astrological traditions are so ancient and widespread as among the Hindus. A birth-chart is made when a child is born and religious propitiations made for unfavourable influences, if any. The earliest and the most religious texts of the Hindus refer to astrology and the faith of an average Hindu in this divine science is strong and unflinching.

The subject, like every other branch of learning is, however, so vast that it is a problem to compress it within a small book. Still an attempt is made here to provide enough guidelines to comprehend the principles of Hindu astrology.

Before dealing with the principles of astrology, we would like to acquaint the beginners with some of the preliminaries, for once they are familiar with the basic background, they would find it easier to follow the subsequent steps.

Zodiac

The earth goes round the Sun but it appears that the Sun goes round the earth. So whether we say the path of the earth or the apparent path of the Sun, it means the same thing. This path is called the ecliptic. The earth's path is strictly on the ecliptic line. The other planets—Mars, Mercury, Jupiter etc. go round the Sun along the ecliptic line, but sometimes they are exactly on this line at others slightly north or south of the ecliptic. This passage is called the zodiac. The Oxford Dictionary defines

---

1. Readers are aware how Julius Ceaser was murdered on the ides of March.

zodiac as "a belt of the heavens limited by lines about 8 degrees from the ecliptic on each side, including all apparent positions of the Sun and planets as known to the ancients and divided into twelve equal parts called signs of the zodiac."

Signs

This zodiac is not exactly circular but elliptic. Since a circle or an ellipse has, as computed from the centre, 360 degrees, each of the twelve parts or sectors constitutes 30 degrees. These twelve sub-divisions are called signs. Why are they called signs? A sign means 'mark traced on surface etc.' and in each of these sub-divisions there are different patterns formed by the fixed stars, so there are different types of marks constituted by the stars or groups of stars and each sub-division is identified by the special pattern formed therein by the fixed stars. These fixed stars or groups of fixed stars are called asterisms or constellations in English and *nakshatra* in Sanskrit. This word *nakshatra* will recur again and again in this book and so the readers would be well-advised to acquaint themselves with this word.

To revert to signs, since the zodiac is divided into twelve parts of 30 degrees each, there are twelve signs named as follows:

1. Aries	5. Leo	9. Sagittarius
2. Taurus	6. Virgo	10. Capricorn
3. Gemini	7. Libra	11. Aquarius
4. Cancer	8. Scorpio	12. Pisces.

Tropical and Sidereal Zodiac

There is only one Sun, one earth and one zodiac. Why are there then two names for the zodiac? This is being explained. If we were to measure a straight line, every one would commence from one end and finish at the other. But when the figure is circular or elliptic, the question arises from where to begin, on the circumference. The Western astronomers commence from that point on the zodiac where the Sun appears to be on or about 21st March—at the spring equinox—when the day and the night are equal. Then, from there they mark sectors of 30 degrees each and call them Aries, Taurus etc. This is called computing in the tropical zodiac.

But this point—the spring equinoctical point—is not fixed or constant. In about 72 years it recedes by about one degree, with the result that if the tropical zodiac commenced at a point, say X in the year 1900, it commenced at a point one degree prior to point X in the year 1972. Thus, this point not being a fixed one, the Hindus rejected it for astrological and predictive purposes and followed the system of commencing the measurement on the zodiac from a fixed star or constellation called *Ashwini* in Sanskrit. The fixed stars or constellations have also some slight motion in thousands of years but that motion being infinitesimal, is for all practical purposes considered negligible. So the Hindus compute the twelve signs from *Ashwini* (a fixed constellation) and divide the zodiac into twelve parts of 30 degrees each and call them Aries, Taurus, Gemini Cancer etc. Since this computing is from a fixed point, it is called the fixed zodiac or the sidereal zodiac. The word sidereal is derived from the Latin word *sidereus* which means pertaining to the constellations (fixed stars).

Since the 0° or the commencing point in the tropical zodiac is ever gradually preceding, the distance between the commencing points on the two zodiacs (the tropical and the sidereal) has accumulated to 23 degrees 29 minutes 4 seconds of the arc on 1st January, 1973. This phenomenon of the precession of the equinoctical point is called precession of the equinoxes. Thus, the readers will observe that the zodiac is one and one only but due to the variation in the commencing points, it is referred to differently as the tropical zodiac and the sidereal zodiac.

Longitudes of Planets

The Hindu astrology is sidereal. All references hereafter are to the sidereal zodiac only. The position of a planet from 0 degree to 360th degree—anywhere on the zodiac is called the longitude.

One degree is divided into 60 minutes. One minute is further

sub-divided into 60 seconds. When we want to be very exact.
We refer not only to the degree but to minutes and seconds
also. The symbols for degree, minutes and seconds are as
follows: 23 degrees, 29 minutes, 4 seconds = 23°-29'-4".
We have explained earlier that each sign extends to 30°. The
domain of each of the signs, is therefore, as follows:

1. Aries	0° to 30°		7. Libra	180° to 210°
2. Taurus	30° to 60°		8. Scorpio	210° to 240°
3. Gemini	60° to 90°		9. Sagittarius	240° to 270°
4. Cancer	90° to 120°		10. Capricorn	270° to 300°
5. Leo	120° to 150°		11. Aquarius	300° to 330°
6. Virgo	150° to 180°		12. Pisces	330° to 360°

The Sanskrit names for the twelve signs are as follows:

1. *Mesha*	5. *Simha*	9. *Dhanu*
2. *Vrisha*	6. *Kanya*	10. *Makara*
3. *Mithuna*	7. *Tula*	11. *Kumbha*
4. *Karka*	8. *Vrischika*	12. *Meena*

The readers will do well to memorise these names of the
twelve signs. There will be references to these names again and
again in this text-book. Now, please note one more point in
this connection. Suppose a planet is in the 36th degree of the
zodiac. You may refer to it as being in the 36th degree or as
occupying the 6th degree of Taurus, because the sign Aries
finishes at 30° and the 36th degree would be 6th degree in
Taurus. Or take another example. Suppose a planet's longitude
is 242°-15'. Now looking to the above table you know that
Scorpio finishes at 240°—so the planet's longitude will be 2°-
15' in the next sign i.e., Sagittarius. Since 8 signs have been
completed, we refer to the planet's longitude as 8-2°-15'. Here
8 stands for the completed sign—Scorpio, which is the 8th sign
in the zodiac. So there are two methods prevalent in referring
to the longitude of a planet. Either you say 242°-15' or you refer
to it as 8-2°-15'—it means the same thing. We shall in this book
follow the second method, because it obviates the necessity of
dividing the number of degrees by 30 and determining the
sign position.

Planets

The Hindu astrology takes cognisance of only nine planets: (1) Sun, (2) Moon, (3) Mars, (4) Mercury, (5) Jupiter, (6) Venus, (7) Saturn, (8) Rahu and (9) Ketu. It does not deal with Uranus (also called Herschel), Neptune and Pluto. The Sanskrit names for the planets are as follows:

1. *Ravi or Surya*	6. *Shukra*
2. *Chandra*	7. *Shani*
3. *Mangal or Kuja*	8. *Rahu and*
4. *Budha*	9. *Ketu.*
5. *Guru or Brihaspati*	

Strictly speaking, the Sun and the Moon are luminaries. Mars, Mercury, Jupiter, Venus and Saturn are planets. Rahu and Ketu are the northern and the southern nodes of the Moon. Where the Moon in its orbit round the earth cuts the ecliptic and goes to the north of it, the point is called the northern node of the Moon and the corresponding position, where the Moon cuts the ecliptic and goes south of it, is called the southern node of the Moon. These two positions on the ecliptic are always 180° apart. These positions are, however, not fixed but are receding month to month so that in a period of about 19 years they complete one cycle of the zodiac. Since these points recede they always have a backward motion. These points besides being referred to as the nodes of the Moon are in English referred to as Caput Draconis and Cauda Draconis. We shall, however, refer to them as Rahu and Ketu in this text-book. These are merely sensitive points but have a powerful influence on the human beings. The Hindu scholars, therefore, have included them in astrological calculations. As explained above these are not planets but for convenience, the Sun, the Moon, Mars.....Saturn, Rahu and Ketu are all referred to as planets. In Sanskrit all the nine are called *grahas*. The word literally means that which holds or attracts and thereby exerts influence.

CHAPTER II

THE BIRTH CHART

We have discussed in the earlier chapter that the positions of the stars and the planets at the time of birth of a person influence him. Just as on a photographic plate when exposed is etched the imprint of the objects before it, so too the child as soon as it comes out of the mother's body is impressed with the various influences at work in the ambient. And we chart these influences on paper to have a record of the longitudes occupied by various planets at that time. We also note the degree of the zodiac rising at the east at the place of birth. Why is it necessary to note the zodiacal longitude at the east—at the place of birth? This is, because that helps us to determine the relative positions of the planets *vis-a-vis* the place of birth. We shall explain this further.

The earth is always rotating on its axis and completes one rotation in 24 hours and this causes the phenomenon of day and night. During this period of 24 hours the various zodiacal signs rise in the east one after the other. Barring the polar regions, all the twelve signs of the zodiac in the regular order Aries, Taurus etc. rise in the east. The duration of rise of the various signs differs from latitude (geographical) and also according as the birth place, for which computation is made, is above the equator or below it. (North or South of the equator).

The Sun's motion in one day *i.e.,* twenty-four hours is on an average about one degree. It is reiterated that the Sun does not move; it is the earth which moves. But in common parlance we say the Sun rises, the Sun sets and so on and similarly in astrology we refer to the apparent motion of the Sun as simply the Sun's motion. To revert to the subject, on a particular day say at 12 noon Greenwich Mean Time the Sun has stepped into the first degree of Aries. Now for 24 hours he would remain in the 1ˢᵗ degree. So in all birth charts of children— born anywhere on earth the Sun would be shown in the 1ˢᵗ degree of Aries. But at a particular time say when it is noon at London, the Sun will be high up in the mid-heaven there but in India he will be setting and in the U.S.A. he would be rising. Thus, the Sun at a particular time forms different angels with the various geographical regions on earth. And what has been stated in respect of the Sun applies *mutatis mutandis* to other planets also.

It is to record the position of the planets in relation to the place of birth, that the zodiacal degree at the eastern horizon is recorded. Suppose, the 1ˢᵗ degree of Aries is rising at the east. Then sign Aries will extend upto the 30th degree below the horizon, then for another 30 degrees below the horizon will be sign Taurus, then Gemini, then Cancer and so on. All these signs will be below the earth. The count is made in the regular order Aries, Taurus, Gemini etc. anticlockwise *i.e., via* below the earth.

Since a circle has 360 degrees, half of this *i.e.,* 180 degrees covers the sector of the heavens from east to west below the earth and the other 180 degrees cover the sector of the heavens west to east above the earth, so that the distance between the zodiacal degree rising at the east is always 180 degrees distant from the zodiacal degree setting at the west.

In the above example, since the first degree Aries is rising in the east, 1ˢᵗ degree of Libra (from the first degree Aries to the first degree Libra, it will be exactly 180 degrees) would be on the western horizon. Then from this zodiacal degree in the west to 30th degree above the western horizon (towards east) will be Libra, then Scorpio then Sagittarius, then Capricorn then Aquarius, then Pisces and the first degree of Aries on the eastern horizon—from where we had started.

Suppose the sign Virgo is rising at the eastern horizon. Then Libra will be below it—under the earth, followed by Scorpio,

Sagittarius, Capricorn and Aquarius—all below the earth; Pisces would be at the western horizon and proceeding from west to east Aries, Taurus, Gemini, Cancer and Leo would be above the earth to complete the circle at Virgo at the eastern horizon.

After some time, the sign Virgo would go up and Libra would rise at the eastern horizon. In fact, it is due to the rotation of the earth on its axis that the sign at the western horizon appears to go up, but in common parlance we say that the sign goes up or rises. So the sign at the eastern horizon is called the rising sign. The particular degree of the zodiac—actually at the eastern horizon is called the rising degree. Because after some time it goes higher up *i.e.*, it ascends, so it is called the ascendant also and the particular degree at the eastern horizon is called the ascending degree. The rising sign and the ascendant mean the same thing. The rising degree or the ascending degree also mean the same thing.

Please always remember that:

(*i*) The count of signs is always made in the regular order Aries, Taurus etc.

(*ii*) We commence from the eastern horizon proceed *via* below the earth upto the western horizon and then from west to east above the horizon.

Calculation of the Birth Chart

For calculating the ascending degree we must have the following particulars:

(*i*) The longitude and the latitude of the place of birth.
(*ii*) Date of birth.
(*iii*) Local mean time of birth.

The longitude of the birth place is required to convert the standard or civil time into local mean time. The latitude of the birth place is required because the duration of rising of each sign differs from latitude to latitude. A regular book called Tables of Houses furnishes the duration of each sign rising at each latitude. We shall have occasion to refer to it later in this very chapter.

The date (date, month and year) of birth is necessary to know the sidereal time at the preceding noon. All modern ephemerides furnish the sidereal time at noon each day.

It would be easier to explain the mapping of the birth chart by taking a specific example. Suppose a child is born on Wednesday the 6th December, 1972 at Delhi at 10-15 p.m. Indian standard time. The ascending degree of the zodiac at the eastern horizon at the place of birth, at birth time is calculated on the basis of the local mean time. So the first step is to convert the standard time into local mean time. For this we proceed as follows:

Local Mean Time

Ascertain the central meridian of the country or the State on the basis of which the standard time has been fixed. The Indian standard time has been fixed for 82°-30' East because 82°-30' when multiplied by 4 (4 minutes of time for each degree) yields 5 hours 30 minutes, which is the difference between the Indian standard time and Greenwich mean time. The Greenwich mean time has been fixed for 0° longitude. Since the longitude 82°-30' east is to the east of Greenwich, the Indian standard time is 5 hours 30 minutes ahead of Greenwich mean time so that when it is 12 noon G.M.T. it is 5-30 p.m. I.S.T. Now, in the present example the birth was at Delhi. Delhi's longitude is 77°-13' east. Deducting 77°-13' from 82°-30'—the central meridian of India—we get 5°-17'. Multiplying the degrees by four minutes 5×4=20. We get 20 minutes and the 17' by four seconds[1] we get 68 seconds or 1 minutes, 8 seconds. Adding this to 20 minutes we get 21 minutes 8 seconds which is the difference between the Indian standard time and the local mean time at Delhi. Because Delhi is west of 82°-30'—the central meridian of India—local mean time at Delhi will be less than the standard time *i.e.*, 9-53-52 p.m.

But what to do if you do not know to which central meridian the standard time of your country conforms? We are providing

---

1. Multiply each ° by 4 minutes, and each second of arc by 4 seconds.

an alternate method of finding the local mean time. For example, in the United States of America there were different standard times—for different zones—the Eastern standard time, the Central standard time, Mountain standard time and the Pacific standard time. These four times were respectively five, six, seven and eight hours behind the Greenwich mean time.

At present in the U.S.A. there are seven time zones: (*i*) the Eastern time, (*ii*) the Central time, (*iii*) the Mountain time, (*iv*) the Pacific time, (*v*) the Yokon time, (*vi*) the Alaska or the Hawaiian time and, (*vii*) the Berring time. These are respectively 5, 6, 7, 8, 9, 10, and 11 hours behind the Greenwich mean time.

To revert to the alternate method of converting the standard time into local mean time in the example horoscope the baby was born at Delhi at 10-15 p.m. I.S.T.[1] Convert it in to G.M.T.,[2] by deducting 5 hours 30 minutes from it which comes to 4-45 p.m. G.M.T. Now, since Delhi's longitude is 77°-13' multiplying the degrees by 4 minutes and the 13 minutes by 4 seconds, we get 308 minutes 52 seconds or 5 hours 8 minutes 52 seconds. Add this to G.M.T. 4-45 p.m. and we get 9-53-52 p.m. as the L.M.T.[3]

Why have we added 5-8-52 to G.M.T.? Because Delhi is east of Greenwich. Please always remember that the time in the west is always less and in the east, it is always more.

So by whichever method we convert the I.S.T. into L.M.T., in the example horoscope we get 9-53-52 p.m. as L.M.T.

Sidereal Time at Preceding Noon

The sidereal time or the star time means that if you set a special clock at 0 hour 0 minute 0 second, at the moment the Sun enters the spring equinoctical point (*i.e.*, tropical sign of Aries), the clock time will show exactly 24 hours at the commencement of the next year. Thus, over and above the normal time registered by an ordinary clock, the sidereal clock accelerates at the rate of about 3 minutes 56 seconds per day so that it will be fast at

---

1. Indian standard time.
2. Greenwich mean time.
3. Local mean time.

next noon by about 3 minutes 56 seconds. The sidereal time at noon provides us the data as to how far the Sun has travelled from the initial point in zodiac. The daily sidereal time at noon is furnished in all modern ephemerides.

In the example horoscope the birth was on 6th December, 1972. Looking up Raphael's ephemeris for 1972 we find that the sidereal time at noon on 6th December at Greenwich was 17 hours 1 minute 29 seconds. But this was the sidereal time at noon at Greenwich and we have to find the sidereal time at noon at Delhi, so we deduct 51 seconds from it and the sidereal time at noon at Delhi would be 17 hours 0 minute 38 seconds.

Please remember, for calculating local mean time if the birth place is east of Greenwich (for example, India) we *add* to Greenwich mean time but for calculating sidereal time we *deduct* from the sidereal time at Greenwich noon. Why do we deduct in the latter case and not add ? Because at Delhi the noon will be about 5 hours 8 minutes 52 seconds earlier and since the acceleration in sidereal time is 9.8 seconds (or roughly 10 seconds) per hour, when it is 12 noon of local mean time at Delhi, it will be 6-51-8 a.m. Greenwich mean time and naturally less than at 12 G.M.T. noon. A good formula to remember as to how many seconds are to be deducted from G.M.T. noon sidereal time is : Multiply the longitude of the place of birth by 2 and divide the product by 3 or say the number of seconds will be two thirds of longitude. These number of seconds are deducted from or added G.M.T. noon sidereal time, according as the place of birth is to the east or west of Greenwich.

Sidereal Time at Birth

Once we have ascertained the sidereal time at the preceding noon, it is easy to find the sidereal time at birth. Please remember that the calculation for the sidereal time of birth is always made on the basis of (*i*) sidereal time at preceding noon and (*ii*) the local mean time of birth and *not* the standard time (or watch time) of birth. In the example, we have found that (*i*) the sidereal time at birth at preceding noon was 17 hours 0 minute 38 seconds and (*ii*) the local mean time was 9-53-52 p.m. or say

9 hours 53 minutes 52 seconds after local mean noon.

Now to calculate the sidereal time of birth, we proceed as follows:

		Hrs.	Mts.	Secs.
(*i*)	Sidereal time at preceding noon.	17	0	38
(*ii*)	Local mean time of birth (time elapsed since noon).	9	53	52
(*iii*)	Add acceleration at 9.8 seconds per hour for (*ii*) above.	0	1	37
(*iv*)	Sidereal time at birth When the total is more than 24 hours, deduct	26	56	7
	24 hours.	24	0	0
		2	56	7

Thus, 2 hours 56 minutes 7 seconds is the sidereal time at birth. It is also called the right ascension of the meridian cusp or R.A.M.C.

Longitude Rising at the East

After calculating the sidereal time at birth, we require *Tables of Houses* to find the longitude rising at the east. What is Tables of Houses ? It is a book specifying the sign, degree and minute, rising at various sidereal times at different latitudes (geographical). Most of the astrologers use Raphael's Tables of Houses published by W. Foulsham & Co. Ltd. of London. The book is available all over the world.

The place of birth in the example horoscope is Delhi. Delhi's latitude is 28°-39' North. So we look up the page giving the sign, degree and minute rising at this latitude. The relevant excerpt from the page is being given below:

Excerpt from Raphael's Tables of Houses
(page giving the rising degrees for Delhi)

Hrs.	Mts.	Secs.	Sign	Degree	Minute
2	54	7	4	19	31
2	58	7	4	20	22

It does not give the sign, degree and minute for 2 hours 56 minutes 7 seconds—which is the sidereal time in the example horoscope. So, by rule of three we calculate and find that for 2 hours 56 minutes 7 seconds the rising sign, degrees, minutes and seconds would be 4 signs (completed) 19 degrees 56 minutes 30 seconds.

The Raphael's Tables of Houses, however, gives the position in the tropical zodiac, while in Hindu astrology we have to find the sign, degrees, minutes and seconds in the sidereal zodiac.

Ascendant in the Sidereal Zodiac

In order to convert the tropical co-ordinates into the sidereal ones we have to deduct the precession of equinox from the former.

	S	D	M	S[1]
Sign rising in the tropical zodiac	4	19	56	30
Deduct precession of equinoxes on birth date.		23	28	59
Sign rising in the sidereal zodiac (Hindu System)	3	26	27	31

One sign has 30 degrees; one degree has 60 minutes; One minute has 60 seconds.

Since 3 represents—3 signs completed *i.e.*, Aries, Taurus, Gemini—the fourth sign Cancer is rising and the rising degree is 26° 27' 31". In the above calculations we have gone to the extent of seconds. It is, however, quite sufficient, if we knock off the seconds, rounding them to the nearest minute. We now make the chart as follows:

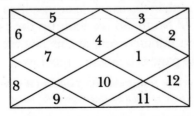

This is the pattern of chart used in northern and western India. We shall at a subsequent stage familiarise our readers with other patterns used in southern and eastern India.

----

1. *SDMS* stand for signs, degrees, minutes and seconds respectively.

Before proceeding on further, we would like to explain from where we have taken this figure of 23° 28' 59" as the value of the precession of equinoxes on 6th December, 1972. Our purpose is to explain each step so that a beginner does not find a dark alley anywhere.

The Hindu ephemerides give the value of the precession on the first of each month and by rule of three the exact value can be calculated for any intervening date.

The *Hindu Predictive Astrology* by Pandit Gopesh Kumar Ojha gives a table of precession of equinoxes on the first of each year from 1880 to 1972. At the end of this book we are giving an abridged table. The exact value for any intervening date can be found by interpolation.

Signs in Other Houses

In Raphael's Tables of Houses the signs and degrees which are to be put in other houses have been provided. But in Hindu astrology no cognisance is taken of these. We have to ascertain the sign and degree of the ascendant or the first house and then subsequent signs are placed on 2nd, 3rd........ 12th houses in regular order. Instead of putting Aries, Taurus etc., we put numerals. 1 means Aries, 2 means Taurus and so on.

Signs and Houses

The top centre indicated by the numeral 4 indicates that the fourth sign of the zodiac is rising or is the ascendant. 5 refers to Leo, 6 refers to Virgo, 7 to Libra and so on. Refer to page 4.

Now, Cancer constitutes the first house. The rising sign is synonymous with the ascendant or the first house. Leo constitutes the second house, Virgo the third, Libra the fourth, Scorpio the fifth, Sagittarius the sixth, Capricorn the seventh, Aquarius the eight, Pisces the ninth, Aries the tenth, Taurus the eleventh and Gemini the twelfth.

The twelve houses from the ascendant—the ascendant always being the first house—are constituted by the twelve signs—counted in the regular order from the sign on the first house. It is very important to understand the nomenclature of *house* because we shall have to refer to houses again and again in this book. We shall explain in subsequent chapters what each house stands for—which matters are to be judged from each house—how planets situated in various houses affect our various departments of life and other vital matters connected with astrology.

Suppose Aquarius is the rising sign or the ascendant or the first house; then Pisces will constitute the second house, Aries the third house and so on. Suppose Virgo is the rising sign, then Virgo will constitute the first house, Libra the second, Scorpio the third.......and Leo the twelfth.

Placing Planets in Signs

The next step is to put planets in signs in the birth chart. The sidereal ephemerides giving daily longitudes of planets will show at a glance in which sign each planet is on a particular day. The ephemerides giving longitudes of planets in the tropical zodiac give the planetary positions in the tropical signs. But in order to calculate the actual degree and minute, at a particular hour and minute, we have to calculate by rule of three or by proportional logarithms.

In the example horoscope, the time of birth is 10-15 p.m. Indian standard time on 6th December 1972. This time, as we have shown earlier is equivalent to 4-45 p.m. Greenwich Mean Time. So, if you want to calculate the longitude of planets from Raphael's ephemeris you have to calculate it for 4-45 p.m. G.M.T. because the Raphael's ephemeris gives longitudes for 12 Noon Greenwich mean time everyday.

We shall work out below longitudes of planets for 4-45 p.m. G.M.T. equivalent to 10-15 Indian standard time.

Longitudes of planets as given for 12 noon G.M.T.		Daily Motion
	S. D. M. S.	D. M. S.
Sun	8-14-28-41	1- 0-58
Moon	8-21-31- 8	11-53- 2
Mars	7-13-41- 0	0-41- 0
Mercury	7-26-18- 0	0-13- 0
Jupiter	9-12- 2- 0	0-13- 0
Venus	7-14-45- 0	1-15- 0
Saturn	2-17-19- 0 R	0- 5- 0
Rahu	9-18-36- 0 R	0- 3-11

The longitudes of planets at 12 Greenwich mean noon, as given above have been taken from the Raphael's Ephemeris for 1972. This ephemeris in previous years used to give longitudes for 12 noon G.M.T. now it gives for E.T.[1] The difference between G.M.T. and E.T. in 1972 is 42 seconds only and for all practical purposes the longitudes given above may be taken for 12 noon G.M.T.

How do we know the daily motion of planets ? We can ascertain this by knowing the position of a planet today at 12 noon and tomorrow at 12 noon. The difference between the two would be the daily motion (*i.e.,* motion in 24 hours) of the planet.

Retrograde Planets

The readers will have observed that against Saturn and Rahu we have written R above. What does R mean ? R means that the planet is retrograde. The Sun and the Moon have always forward motion; Rahu and Ketu have always backward (retrograde) motion. The rest five—Mars, Mercury, Jupiter, Venus and Saturn have generally forward motion and at times retrograde. Actually, they in their orbit round the Sun move forward, but an illusion is created, when viewed from the earth, that they are receding backward.

Suppose you are going in a fast car. You look backward at a cyclist who is also going in the same direction in which you are proceeding. But due to your much faster motion, the distance between you and the cyclist goes on increasing and an illusion is created that the cyclist is moving backward. Some such phenomenon gives us the impression that the planet is retrograde or receding backwards. You have the longitudes of the planets at 12 noon G.M.T. And you have to find the longitudes of planets at 4-45 p.m. G.M.T. (equivalent to 10-15 p.m. I.S.T.). So you have to calculate the motion for 4 hours 45 minutes and add it to the longitudes at 12 noon G.M.T. in case of planets having forward motion (called direct in astrology) but subtract it from the 12 noon G.M.T. longitudes in case of retrograde planet.

The ephemeris gives longitudes of planets upto degrees, minutes and seconds in case of the Sun and the Moon. In case

---

1. E.T.—Ephemeris time.

of others, the longitudes have been given upto degrees and minutes only. In advanced Hindu astrology, longitudes of all the planets is calculated upto degrees, minutes and seconds, but for all practical purposes, it would do if you eliminate seconds.

Motion in 4 Hours 45 Minutes

There are two methods of calculation. One is by the rule of three and the other is by logarithms. The method of calculating by proportional logarithms has been given in Raphael's Ephemeris and also in Lahiris Indian Ephemeris and is not being repeated. Readers have, it is expected an elementary knowledge of the rule of three as applied in arithmetic and so we are not explaining here the same either.

The motion of the various planets for 4 hours 45 minutes would be as follows:

	D. M. S.		D. M. S.
Sun	0-12- 4	Jupiter	0- 2-34
Moon	2-21-56	Venus	0-14-51
Mars	0- 8- 6	Saturn	0- 0- 1
Mercury	0- 2-34	Rahu	0- 0- 1

In calculating the above fractions have been rounded off, because it is not of practical use to put decimal points after seconds.

Tropical Longitudes at Birth Time

Adding these motions to the longitudes of planets at 12 noon G.M.T., we arrive at the longitudes at 4-45 p.m. But in case of Saturn and Rahu—since these were retrograde, we have to subtract from the longitude at 12 noon G.M.T. The result is as follows:

	S.D.M.S.		S.D.M.S.
Sun	8-14-40-45	Jupiter	9-12- 4-34
Moon	8-23-53- 4	Venus	7-14-59-51
Mars	7-13-49- 6	Saturn	2-17-18- 0
Mercury	7-26-20-34	Rahu	9-18-35- 0

But all these are the longitudes in the tropical zodiac. In order to reduce them to longitudes in the sidereal zodiac we have to deduct the precession of equinoxes from each of these, as we did in case of the rising sign (ascendant).

	S. D. M. S.
Thus, Sun's tropical longitude	8-14-40-45
Less precession of equinox	0-23-28-59
Sun's sidereal longitude	
	7-21-11-46

Sidereal Longitudes at Birth Time

By following the above method in case of each of the planets we get the following longitudes of planets in the sidereal zodiac. The longitudes have been rounded off to the nearest minute. The seconds have been knocked off. It is not necessary to calculate upto seconds.

	S.D.M.		S.D.M.
Sun	7-21-12	Venus	6-21-31
Moon	8- 0-24	Saturn	1-23-49
Mars	6-20-20	Rahu	8-25- 6
Mercury	7- 2-52	Ketu	2-25- 6
Jupiter	8-18-36		

Longitude of Ketu

Some of the readers, who are not acquainted with astrology will be puzzled as to from where we have imported the longitude of Ketu. It is, therefore, necessary to explain that Ketu and Rahu are the two extremes of the same pole diametrically opposite to each other. They are always 180 degrees apart. Since each sign has 30 degrees, 180 divided by 30 yields 6 signs. So in other words, if we add 6 signs to Rahu's longitude we automatically have Ketu's position. In the above example Rahu's longitude is 8-25° -6' . Adding 6 signs it becomes 14-25°-6°'.

When the number of signs comes to more than 12 always deduct 12. Deducting 12 from signs (the degrees and minutes well remain unaltered) we get 2-25°-6' which is the longitude of Ketu we have put above.

Planets in Birth Chart

Now, what remains is to put the planets in the birth chart. The Sun has completed 7 signs and has travelled 21° in the 8th. So we put the Sun where we have put 8 in the figure. The Moon has completed 8 signs and is in 9th so we put the Moon alongside of 9 and so on. Readers are reminded that 1, 2, 3, 4 etc.—the numerals—stand for Aries, Taurus, Gemini, Cancer etc. counted in the regular order.

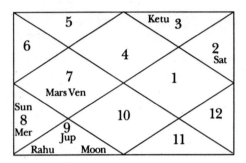

This is the pattern followed in the northern and western India, where in the top centre we put the ascending sign, indicating it by the numeral.

In southern India, the pattern of chart used is different. The place marked with an asterisk is always reserved for Aries and then the twelve signs follow *clockwise*. The planets are put in the signs they are in and the sign rising or the ascendant is noted by putting L (L stands for Lagnam—the Sanskrit word for ascendant) there. Thus, this chart would be written in the south Indian style as follows:

	*	Sat	Ketu
			Asc. (L)
Jup Moon Rahu	Sun Mer	Mars Ven	

In eastern India, a different pattern is used. Here also the place marked with an asterisk is always reserved for Aries but unlike as in south India, the count—Aries, Taurus, Gemini etc.—is made *anticlockwise*.

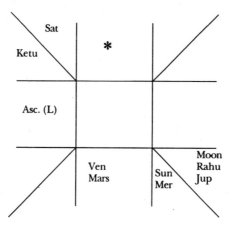

Now, having completed the birth chart, let us recapitulate the main features. The ascendant Cancer is rising; Mars and Venus are in Libra in the fourth house; the Sun and Mercury are in Scorpio in the fifth house; the Moon, Jupiter and Rahu are in Sagittarius in the sixth house; Saturn is in Taurus in the eleventh house and Ketu in Gemini in the twelfth.

In astrological terminology, we do not always use the word house but it is understood. When we say the Moon is in sixth it means 'the Moon is in the sixth house' When we say Saturn is in eleventh, it means, 'Saturn is in the eleventh house' and so on.

While concluding this chapter, we would like to invite the attention of the readers to the following points:

(*i*) The ascendant is always calculated on the basis of the *local mean time* of birth, which in its turn is computed on the basis of the longitude of the birth place, but the longitudes of planets is for the *standard time* and not the *local mean time*.

(*ii*) Once the sidereal time of birth, also called the right ascension of the meridian cusp is calculated, the degree rising at the east—called the ascending degree (the sign in which the ascending degree falls being called the ascendant or the rising sign) must be looked up in the Tables of Houses on the page giving the rising sign for the latitude of birth place. If there is no table identical for the latitude of the birth place, the rising degree should be calculated by interpolation on the basis of the tables for the latitudes between which the latitude of the birth place lies. For example, the Raphael's Tables of Houses is for degrees 27°-10' and 28°-40'. If now the geographical latitude of the birth place is say 27°-55' we have to calculate the ascendant for 27°-10' and 28°-40' and then find by rule of three, as to what will be the ascending degree at latitude 27°-55'.

(*iii*) The Tables of Houses by Raphael is for northern latitudes. If you have to find the ascendant for a place having southern latitude the procedure, has been explained in the Tables of Houses and is, therefore, not being repeated.

(*iv*) If you are using Raphael's ephemeris or Raphael's Tables of Houses or any other western ephemeris or Tables of Houses, which are for the tropical zodiac, you must deduct the precession of equinoxes to reduce the figures to the sidereal zodiac. The Hindu system is on the basis of the sidereal zodiac. For making birth charts of persons born in India we would strongly recommend Lahiri's Indian Ephemeris and Lahiri's Tables of Ascendants which are on the basis of the sidereal zodiac and the readers will be saved the inconvenience of deducting the precession of equinoxes from the rising degree and the longitudes of planets. For readers knowing Hindi, I would recommend a very good Tables of Houses called *Bharatiya lagna Sarini*. This is also for the sidereal zodiac.

(*v*) The readers should take care not to confuse between signs and houses. Signs are Aries, Taurus, Gemini.... Pisces. The houses are first, second, third.....twelfth.

Suppose a giant wheel having twelve spokes is rotating. The twelve spokes divide the cirumference into twelve sectors. Now, let us say, we write the names of the signs—Aries, Taurus, Gemini etc. anticlockwise on the twelve sectors,. The wheel is rotating—clockwise. The mutual positions of the signs (sectors) do not change but due to rotation sometimes some sector comes to the east, sometimes to the other. The sectors as counted from the east are called houses so that when sector Aries is to the east, the fifth house (the fifth sign from Aries) falls in Leo. But if, say the sector Scorpio rises to the east, the fifth house (the fifth house from Scorpio) falls in Pisces. It is very important to understand this difference, for we will have a lot to do with signs and houses in subsequent chapters.

CHAPTER III

SIGNS

To understand astrology we must have an idea of the
characteristics of signs and essential particulars in regard to
them: The signs are twelve. Seven planets are considered rulers
or lords of the signs as per details given below:

	Sign	Lord		Sign	Lord
1.	Aries	Mars	7.	Libra	Venus
2.	Taurus	Venus	8.	Scorpio	Mars
3.	Gemini	Mercury	9.	Sagittarius	Jupiter
4.	Cancer	Moon	10.	Capricorn	Saturn
5.	Leo	Sun	11.	Aquarius	Saturn
6.	Virgo	Mercury	12.	Pisces	Jupiter

Rahu and Ketu are not lords of any sign. It has already been
stated earlier that the Hindu astrology does not take cognisance
of Herschel (Uranus), Neptune or Pluto.

When we have to judge a matter—how far affairs pertaining
to that department in the life of a person would go well or go
wrong, we refer to a particular house and a particular planet in
the birth chart—whether they (the house and the planet) are
strong or weak, whether they are well disposed or ill disposed.
All these matters—what each house stands for—what matters it
governs and in addition to the relevant house, to which other
planet or planets in the chart we must look for, will be dealt
with in subsequent chapters. Here, what we want to impress is
that the readers should know and commit to memory the
names of the twelve signs and which planet is lord of a particular
sign. For in the matter of judgment, when you look to the sign
on a house, you must look to its lord also simultaneously. The

judgment in regard to a sign (and by implication, to the house on which it falls) and its lord cannot be isolated. In the example horoscope worked out in chapter II, Cancer constitutes the ascendant or the first house and its lord is the Moon; Leo constitutes the second house and its lord is the Sun; Virgo falls on the third house and its lord is Mercury: Libra goes to fourth house and its lord is Venus and so on.

So, it is very necessary to remember which planet is the lord of which sign. Suppose Aries falls in the tenth house (as in the example horoscope) then because Mars is the lord of Aries, Mars becomes the lord of the tenth house. In astrological parlance we do not repeat the argument that because Aries falls on the tenth house therefore Mars is the lord of the tenth house. That is astrological terminology, with which readers should become familiar. Now, in the example horoscope Mars is in Libra and Libra constitutes the fourth house in this chart. So we do not say 'because Mars is in Libra which falls on the fourth house so Mars is in the fourth house', but just say 'Mars in fourth' sometimes astrologers use still abbreviated language and say 'lord of tenth in fourth,.

All this is to familiarise readers with a part of astrological terminology. Now, we revert to give some characteristics of signs, which would be useful for better understanding of the subsequent text.

Movable, Fixed and Common Signs

The twelve signs have been divided into three groups of movable, fixed and common signs. Aries, Cancer, Libra and Capricorn are movable ; Taurus, Leo, Scorpio and Aquarius are fixed; Gemini, Virgo, Sagittarius and Pisces are common *i.e.,* having the qualities of movable as well as of fixed signs as we are explaining below:

The movable signs are active and dynamic while the fixed signs are comparatively inactive and static. The first 15 degrees of common signs have the characteristics of fixed signs while the last 15 degrees, those of movable signs.

Person at whose birth a movable sign is rising are active, fond of change and movement and prefer walking while those with a fixed sign rising are thoughtful, reserved and comparatively speaking, of sendentary habits.

Planets in movable, fixed and common signs also reflect the above characteristics.

Odd and Even Signs

Aries, Gemini, Leo, Libra, Sagittarius and Aquarius are called odd signs. Taurus, Cancer, Virgo, Scorpio, Capricorn and Pisces are even signs.

The odd signs represent pushing and aggressive nature, while the even ones passive and docile temperament.

Male and Female Signs

The odd signs are male. The even signs are female.

Signs and Parts of Human Body

The twelve signs Aries to Pisces represent the twelve parts of the human body as follows[1]:

Sign	Part of Human body	Sign	Part of Human body
Aries	head	Libra	basti
Taurus	face	Scorpio	genitals
Gemini	chest	Sagittarius	thighs
Cancer	heart	Capricorn	knees
Leo	stomach	Aquarius	calves
Virgo	navel	Pisces	feet

Western astrologers include throat and neck under Taurus, but Hindu astrologers assign throat to Gemini. Heart includes the corresponding region on the right side also. The area under the governance of Leo extends upto the naval. If we draw a vertical line from the navel to the genitals (excluding latter) and divide it into two parts—the upper region is controlled by Virgo—the lower called *basti* in Sanskrit, is governed by Libra. Organs of generation including those of excretion come under Scorpio, the thighs and hips under Sagittarius.

What is the purpose served by the above allocation? If any

---

1. See *Saravali* Chapter 3 Verse 5 and *Hora Shastra* Chapter I Verse 4.

sign is afflicted by being occupied or aspected by any malefic planet or if the lord of the sign is weak or conjoined with or aspected by a malefic, the person gets hurt in that part of the body or has some ailment or disease there. Which planets are malefic and which others benefic and how they aspect or which sign they aspect will be explained at length in a subsequent chapter.

Signs and Sub-divisions

We have already stated that a sign has 30 degrees. For astrological judgment a sign is divided into 9 sub-divisions: 30° divided by 9 yields 3°-20'. So that when a sign is sub-divided into 9 parts each part covers the following arc:

(1) 0° to   3°-20' (2)   3°-20' to   6°-40' (3)   6°-40' to 10°
(4) 10° to 13°-20' (5) 13°-20' to 16°-40' (6) 16°-40' to 20°
(7) 20° to 23°-20' (8) 23°-20 to 26°-40' (9) 26°-40' to 30°.

When the nine sub-divisions in a sign end, the subsequent sign is similarly sub-divided and so on, so that the entire zodiac has 12×9 = 108 sub-divisions. These 108 sub-divisions are also named after the 12 signs in the regular order. We are giving below the allocation of the 108 sub-divisions:

Aries :	Aries, Taurus, Gemini, Cancer, Leo, Virgo, Libra, Scorpio and Sagittarius.
Taurus :	Capricorn, Aquarius, Pisces, Aries, Taurus, Gemini, Cancer, Leo and Virgo.
Gemini :	Libra, Scorpio, Sagittarius, Capricorn, Aquarius, Pisces, Aries, Taurus and Gemini.
Cancer :	Cancer, Leo, Virgo, Libra, Scorpio, Sagittarius, Capricorn, Aquarius and Pisces.
Leo :	Aries, Taurus, Gemini, Cancer, Leo, Virgo, Libra, Scorpio and Sagittarius.
Virgo :	Capricorn, Aquarius, Pisces, Aries, Taurus, Gemini, Cancer, Leo and Virgo.
Libra :	Libra, Scorpio, Sagittarius, Capricorn, Aquarius, Pisces, Aries, Taurus and Gemini.
Scorpio :	Cancer, Leo, Virgo, Libra, Scorpio, Sagittarius, Capricorn, Aquarius and Pisces.
Sagittarius :	Aries, Taurus, Gemini, Cancer, Leo, Virgo, Libra, Scorpio and Sagittarius.

Capricorn : Capricorn, Aquarius, Pisces, Aries, Taurus, Gemini, Cancer, Leo and Virgo.

Aquarius : Libra, Scorpio, Sagittarius, Capricorn, Aquarius, Pisces, Aries, Taurus and Gemini.

Pisces : Cancer, Leo, Virgo, Libra, Scorpio, Sagittarius, Capricorn, Aquarius and Pisces.

It will be observed that the allocation of the sub-divisions is the same in the following groups of signs:

(*i*) Aries, Leo, Sagittarius.

(*ii*) Taurus, Virgo, Capricorn.

(*iii*) Gemini, Libra, Aquarius.

(*iv*) Cancer, Scorpio, Pisces.

What is the utility of this sub-division ? If a planet is in its own sub-division, it is deemed strong. For example, say the Moon is in 1° in Pisces. Now from 0° to 3°-20' constitutes the first sub-division. On referring to the above table of sub-divisions, we find that the first sub-division of Pisces falls in Cancer. Now since the Moon is the lord of Cancer, if he is in 1° Pisces, he falls in Cancer sub-division and is deemed strong, because he is in his own sub-division.

The other principle is that if a planet is in the same sub-division as the sign it is called *vargottama*. A *vargottama* planet is deemed as strong as if it were in its own sign. We shall illustrate it by a specific example. Suppose the Sun is in Gemini in the 28th degree. Now 26°40' to 30° in any sign constitutes the ninth sub-division. On referring to the table of sub-divisions in Gemini on pages 30-31 we find that the ninth sub-division in Gemini is Gemini itself. So that the Sun in the 28th degree in Gemini is not only in Gemini sign but Gemini sub-division also. He is, therefore, called *vargottama* and though the Sun is the ruler or lord of Leo and *not* of Gemini, yet on account of his *vargottama* position he is *deemed as strong as if he were in his own sign*[1].

---

1. See *Phala Deepika* Chapter IX Verse 20 and *Hora Shastra* Chapter I Verse 14.

A good rule to remember as to which sub-division in a
sign is *vargottama* has been enunciated by Varaha Mihir :
    "The first sub-division in movable signs, the middle one
is fixed one and the last one in common signs is *vargottama.*"
    The sign is called *rashi* in Sanskrit. And the one ninth sub-
division is called *navansha. Nava* means nine and *ansha* means
part. So *navansha* means one ninth part. This is a very useful
word to remember, because hereafter when we have to refer to
the one ninth sub-division, we shall refer to it as *navansha.*

The Navansha Chart

In all elaborate horoscope made in India, you will come across
the *navansha* chart. In southern India it occupies pride of place
and along with the birth chart (popularly known as the *rashi*
chart where the location of the ascendant and the planets is
shown in signs) a *navansha* chart is furnished.
    We shall explain how to draw it. Let us refer to the example
horoscope worked out in Chapter II.
    The ascending degree is 26°-28' in Cancer which falls in
the 8th *navansha i.e.,* Aquarius (see table of *navanshas* given
on pages 31-32). So the *navansha* sign on the ascendant or
the first house would be Aquarius. The Sun is in 22nd degree
of Scorpio *i.e.,* the seventh *navansha* which falls in Capricorn,
so we put the Sun in Capricorn. The Moon is in 1° in
Sagittarius. The first *navansha* of Sagittarius is Aries, so the
Moon goes to Aries. Mars is in 21° of Libra in the seventh
navansha, which is Aries so we place Mars in Aries; Mercury
occupies the 3rd degree in Scorpio which is the first *navansha*
and falls in Cancer. Jupiter is in the 19th degree of Sagittarius
in the sixth *navansha* which is Virgo, so we put him there.
Venus is in 22nd degree of Libra in the seventh *navansha*
which is Aries. So Venus is put in Aries. Saturn's longitude
is 23°-49' in Taurus. After 23°-20' the eighth *navansha* begins;
so Saturn goes to Leo *navansha.* Rahu is in 26th degree of
Sagittarius. From 23°-20' to 26°-40' is the eighth *navansha.*
Looking up the table of *navanshas* we find that the eight
navansha in Sagittarius falls in Scorpio. So Rahu goes to
Scorpio *navansha.* Ketu occupies 25°-6' in Gemini, again
the eighth *navansha.* The eighth *navansha* in Gemini

falls in Taurus and we put Ketu there. The *navansha* charts in

Ven. Moon Mars	12		10 Sun	
1		11		9
	2 Ketu		8 Rahu	
3	4 Mer.	5 Sat.	6 Jup.	7

	Ven Moon Mars	*	Ketu	
Asc. (L)				Mer
Sun				Sat
	Rahu			Jup

the north Indian and the south Indian styles would be as follows:

We have so far not dealt with the principles of judgment of a birth chart or the delineation of the effects. We shall deal with the matter in subsequent chapters. But in passing, we may state that the *navansha* chart shows the latent potentialities. Pandit Gopesh Kumar Ojha an astrologer of international fame and author of *Hindu Predictive Astrology* states in his book *Sugam Jyotish Praveshika* that if the sign chart is like a tree, the *navansha* is like a fruit. A mango tree may be tall and magnificent yet its fruit may be small and sour, whereas a seemingly dwarf tree of unprepossessing appearance may bear big and tasty fruit.

Diurnal and Nocturnal Signs

Leo, Virgo, Libra, Scorpio, Aquarius and Pisces are diurnal signs. Aries, Taurus, Gemini, Cancer, Sagittarius and Capricorn are nocturnal signs. The diurnal signs are strong during day. The nocturnal signs are strong during night. For day births, planets in diurnal signs are stronger; for night births, planets in nocturnal sign possess more strength.

---

* The place marked with an asterisk is reserved for Aries in the southern India pattern of chart and the count is made clockwise.

Direction

Aries, Leo and Sagittarius pertain to the east, Taurus, Virgo and Capricorn to the south; Gemini, Libra and Aquarius to the west and Cancer, Scorpio and Pisces to the north.

If a sign is strong and well-tenanted, benefit from the respective direction may be expected. If converse is the case, harm or loss may come from that direction.

While undertaking a journey, it is desirable to elect time when a sign pointing to the direction of the journey is rising. Also it is preferable to have the Moon in that sign. Suppose you have to take an important journey to the east. It is preferable to commence journey when Aries, Leo or Sagittarius is rising and when the Moon is in any or the above three signs.

Manner of Rising

Aries, Taurus, Cancer, Sagittarius and Capricorn rise with their hind parts first; Gemini, Leo, Virgo, Libra, Scorpio and Aquarius rise head first, Pisces rises both ways.

The signs rising with hind parts first are malefic and best suited for cruel deeds while the signs rising head first are benefic and more appropriate for good purposes. The sign rising both ways shows mixed tendencies. This is the position, when there is no planet in the sign under consideration. If a malefic tenants a sign rising with hind parts, the planet becomes still more malefic. If a benefic planet tenants such a sign, it loses part of its benefic nature. While in case of signs rising with head first, a benefic planet occupying such a sign becomes still more benefic while a malefic loses part of its malevolence.

Further a planet occupying a sign

(*a*) rising head first shows its effect in the beginning of its period,

(*b*) rising with hind part, manifests its effect at a late stage in its period,

(*c*) bothway—the effect is produced in the middle[1] of the period.

For calculation of periods of planets, readers are referred to Chapter IX.

---

1. See Rudra's Commentary on *Hora Shastra* Pages, 23-34.

CHAPTER IV

HOUSES

We have in the previous chapters introduced the word 'house'. We have also stated that there are twelve houses comprised by the twelve signs. Now, the Sun remains in one sign for one month or so in birth charts of all persons born during a month; say 13th April to 13 May, the Sun will remain in Aries and generate a particular influence peculiar to his tenanting Aries. But for a person born in the morning, the Sun will be in the first house; for a native born at noon, the Sun will be in the tenth house, for evening births the Sun will be in the seventh house and for births at midnight the Sun will be in the fourth.

Due to rotation of the earth on its axis—planets including the Sun—make different angles with the eastern horizon as viewed from the place of birth, and this angle determines the house position of a planet.

Now, why has this feature of house or houses has been introduced in astrology ? Because each house represents some part of the human body, some relation (such as father, mother, brother) and some department of life. And for judgment of a particular matter, we have to take into account the planet owning the house, and the planet or planets tenanting or aspecting the house. How planets aspect a house will be explained in a subsequent chapter, but it is necessary to explain what we mean by 'a planet owning the house'. The expressions 'owner of the house', 'ruler of the the house', 'lord of the house'—all mean the same thing. We have explained earlier how when different signs rise in the eastern horizon, the subsequent signs comprise subsequent houses. When Aries is the rising sign, the fourth sign from Aries i.e., Cancer constitutes the fourth house. Now since the Moon is the lord or ruler of Cancer we say the Moon is the lord of the fourth house. Suppose Taurus is the rising sign then—Taurus, Gemini, Cancer, Leo—the fourth house will have the sign Leo on it and we shall say that the Sun, the ruler of Leo, is the ruler or lord of the fourth house.

Thus, it will be observed that the Sun and the Moon will be the lords of one house each (because they own one sign each) but Mars, Mercury, Jupiter, Venus and Saturn will be the lords of two houses each, because each of these five planets owns two signs. Since Rahu and Ketu do not own any sign they do not become lords of *any house*.

Nomenclature for Houses

(*i*)   The first, fourth, seventh and the tenth houses are called angles. Planets herein are deemed to be strong.

(*ii*)   The second, fifth, eighth and the eleventh houses are called succedent houses. Planets herein except the eighth are deemed fairly strong but not so strong as in the angles.

(*iii*) The third, sixth, ninth and the twelfth are called cadent houses. Planets herein except the ninth are considered weak. But malefics in the sixth are deemed to be well-placed. Which ones are malefic planets and which others benefic will be discussed in the next chapter.

(*iv*)   The fifth and the ninth houses are called trines. Lords of trines and planets placed therein are considered good and strong.

The Sanskrit names for (*i*) angles, (*ii*) succedent, (*iii*) cadent and (*iv*) trine houses respectively are (*i*) *kendra,* (*ii*) *panaphara,* (*iii*) *apoklima* and (*iv*) *trikona.*

(*v*)   The third, sixth, tenth and eleventh houses are called *upachaya* houses. *Upachya* is a Sanskrit word meaning increase.

(*vi*)   The sixth, eighth and twelfth houses are called *Trik. Trik* is a Sanskrit word. It means the three evil ones. Planets placed therein and planets which are lords thereof are not considered good.

All the affairs of the world—health, wealth, intelligence,

learning, happiness, misery, spiritual advancement, properties, relations, trade and commerce, sex life, sexual enjoyment, power and position, income, voyages, trips, illness, legacies, enemies, etc., come under some house or the other. But it is not possible to provide too detailed a list of matters governed by each house. So we are succinctly stating below the matters for which a particular house should be looked up. It would be observed that certain matters fall under more than one house, and for these more than one house must be looked up.

First House

Self, body, physique, physical strength, stamina, pose, appearance, complexion, personality, push and vigour, activity, capacity, temperament, inclinations, health, happiness and misery, longevity, hair and head, fame, standing in society, birth place, mother's father, father's mother etc.

Second House

Face, eyes (particularly the right eye), nose, mouth, teeth and tongue, speaking, power of speech (eloquence), quality of speech (soft or harsh, truthful or false), learning (as evidenced by speaking), food, taste for food, wealth (movable as opposed to immovable), grain, jewels, precious metals, money, miserliness in spending, purchase and sale of goods, family members, death etc.

Third House

Throat, voice, ear, power of hearing, shoulders, arms, upper part of the chest, brothers, and sisters (particularly afterborns) companions, relations, neighbours, servants, subordinates and assistants, courage, fight, anger, patience, physical and mental prowess, skill, enterprise, sports, wandering about, short journeys, short writings, longevity, religion etc.

Fourth House

Heart and the corresponding region on the right side, mother, relations—paternal as well as maternal—friends, residential house, land, gardens, agricultural farms, wet lands and produce therefrom cattle, underground water, wells and tanks, comforts, sleeping, happiness, reputation, sweet smell, conveyances, education (according to south Indian school), piety, moral virtues, termination of things, end of life etc.

Fifth House

Belly, pregnancy, liver, children—sons and daughters—mind, education, and learning, memory, intelligence, wisdom, advice, long literary production, devotion to God, incantations and prayers, good deeds done in previous births, hereditary post of a minister, good morals, pleasures, liaison with courtesans, speculation, betting, games of chance (gain from gambling, racing) etc.

Sixth House

Parts of body around the navel, lower intestines, pancreas, appendix, maternal uncles and aunts, diseases, hurts, wounds, mental and bodily ailments, worries, enmity, enemies, fighting exertion, calamities, imprisonment, quarrels with brothers, theft, reproach, obstacles and impediments, vice and vicious habits, cruel acts, service, servants, debts etc.

Seventh House

Marriage, husband/wife, lust, sexual intercourse, liaisons with others, matrimonial happiness, description of husband/wife, longevity of married partner, the genitals and urinary tract (interior portion) business partner, trade, partnership business, journey, break in journey, lawsuits, overthrow of enemy, death etc.

Eighth House

Genitals (exterior portion) anus, venereal diseases, also diabetes and spermatorrhoea, piles, fistula, longevity, mental distress, sins, sorrows, calamities, diseases, bad name, ill repute legacy, trouble to wife/husband, brother's enemy, underground money, death, place and manner of death, battle, things across the waters, country house (other than the ancestral house), loss of money, formidable obstructions, punishment from government, fear, defeat etc.

Ninth House

Thighs and hips, father (according to south Indian school), grand children; brother's wife, sister's husband, wife's/husband's brothers and sisters, religious shrines, worship, good deeds, charity, spiritual and philosophical outlook, efforts for acquisition of knowledge, association with good people voyage, general wellbeing, good fortune (covering residential house, wealth, respect and comforts).This is called the house of 'Bhagya'. Bhagya is a Sanskrit word and includes, wealth, happiness and all factors which contribute to good fortune etc.

Tenth House

Knees, back, father (according to north Indian school), mother-in-law, adopted son, service employment, means of livelihood, profession, action, deeds (good or evil), accomplishment, business, success, agriculture, travelling, living abroad, king, government, honour, position, fame or ill fame, rank and status, superiors in authority, renunciation asceticism etc.

Eleventh House

Calves of legs, elder brothers and sisters, son-in-law, daughter-in-law, mother's longevity, income, gain, acquisition, profit and loss, gain from father-in-law, paraphernalia of luxury, vehicles, enemies and matters connected therewith, clothes, paternal wealth, wisdom, skill, learning, desires and fulfilment thereof, worshipping of deities etc.

Twelfth House

Feet, father's younger brother or sister, maternal uncle's wife, mother's sister's husband, comforts of bed (sex indulgence— marital as well as extra marital), loss of wife, self undoing, mental distress, sorrow, imprisonment, mutilation of limb, wretchedness, loss, expenditure (of vital bodily forces as well as of money), purchase of articles of luxury, generosity, wandering far away from homeland, residence abroad, fall from position etc.

In astrology all things—affairs and matters pertaining to the various departments of life—fall under one house or the other and are in the protfolio of one or more planets. About planets we shall deal with in a subsequent chapter. Confining ourselves to the discussion on houses here, we may state that some of our readers may be puzzled to find that some matters are covered by more than one house. We may explain it as follows:

A medical expert may observe that a sound heart is essential for longevity. He may also state that proper digestive functioning is also a 'must' for long life. Further normal blood pressure and normal blood sugar are also essential for long tenure of life. In this manner we find that when we judge bodily health, we have to take several factors into account. So it is in astrology.

CHAPTER V

PLANETS

Having explained the characteristics of signs and what to judge from each of the twelve houses, we are now giving some characteristics of planets.

Which sign is owned by which planet has been stated earlier on page 27 and we shall not repeat the same here. A planet when occupying its own sign is deemed strong. On this principle the Sun in Leo, Moon in Cancer, Mars in Aries or Scorpio, Mercury in Gemini or Virgo, Jupiter in Sagittarius or Pisces, Venus in Taurus or Libra and Saturn in Capricorn or Aquarius are deemed strong. Rahu in Virgo and Ketu in Pisces are deemed well-placed.

Moola-Trikona

The Sanskrit word *Moola-Trikona* in the context of astrology means that a planet in its *Moola-Trikona* sign is deemed in a better position than even being in its own sign. The respective signs and degrees in which a planet is in *Moola-Trikona* are being given below:

Planet	Sign	Degrees
Sun	Leo	0° to 20°
Moon	Taurus	3° to 30°
Mars	Aries	0° to 12°
Mercury	Virgo	15° to 20°
Jupiter	Sagittarius	0° to 10°
Venus	Libra	0° to 5°
Saturn	Aquarius	0° to 20°
Rahu	Aquarius	0° to 30°
Ketu	Leo	0° to 30°

Exaltation

There is yet another category. Planets in the respective signs given below are deemed in exaltation. In a sign, seventh from its exaltation sign, the planet is treated as being in debilitation. A planet in its sign of exaltation is deemed even stronger than in its own sign, while a planet in its sign of debilitation is deemed very weak.

A planet is called exalted when it is in its sign of exaltation, while a planet is called debilitated, if it tenants its sign of debilitation. The following table specifies the respective signs of exaltation and debilitation of the various planets.

Planet	Sign of Exaltation	Sign of Debilitation
Sun	Aries	Libra
Moon	Taurus (0° to 3°)	Scorpio
Mars	Capricorn	Cancer
Mercury	Virgo (0° to 15°)	Pisces
Jupiter	Cancer	Capricorn
Venus	Pisces	Virgo
Saturn	Libra	Aries

It will be observed that the Moon is exalted in the first three degrees in Taurus and is in his *Moola-Trikona* in the other 27 degrees. Mercury is exalted in Virgo in the first fifteen degrees, in his *Moola-Trikona* in the next five degrees and in his own sign in the last ten degrees.

About Rahu and Ketu there is difference of opinion as to which ones are their signs of exaltation. According to one school Rahu is exalted in Gemini and debilitated in Sagittarius; according to the other Rahu is exalted in Taurus and debilitated in Scorpio.

Friendship among Planets

Two kinds of friendship and enmity between planets is taken cognisance of in astrology. The one is the natural and the other temporary. We shall deal with natural relationship first.

Natural Relationship

Planet	Friend	Neutral	Enemy
Sun	Moon Mars Jupiter	Mercury	Venus Saturn
Moon	Sun Mercury	Mars Jupiter Venus Saturn	—
Mars	Sun Moon Jupiter	Venus Saturn	Mercury
Mercury	Sun Venus	Mars Jupiter Saturn	Moon
Jupiter	Sun Moon Mars	Saturn	Mercury Venus
Venus	Mercury Saturn	Mars Jupiter	Sun Moon
Saturn	Mercury Venus	Jupiter	Sun Moon Mars

It will be observed that Mercury is Sun's natural but Sun is Mercury's friend. So, the mutual disposition in all cases is not identical. There are very good reasons for fixing the natural relationship given above, but to explain the theory and the rationale behind it would take more space and we are not going into the same here.

Temporary Relationship

The natural relationship between planets as given above is fixed and applies to all the charts. But the temporary relationship between planets differs from chart to chart. The principle applied in determining the temporary relationship is that:

(*i*) a planet in second, third, fourth, tenth, eleventh and twelfth from it is a friend.

(*ii*) a planet in first, fifth, sixth, seventh, eighth and ninth from it is an enemy.

There are no neutrals here. The count is made from sign to sign. Thus, in the example horoscope, the Sun is in the fifth house. Mercury is in the same house. So the sun and Mercury are enemies. Here the disposition is mutual, that is to say if A is B's enemy then *vice versa* B also is A's enemy. To revert to the example horoscope on page 23 the Moon and Jupiter are in the sixth house. Counted from fifth (were the Sun is posited—and we are determining Sun's friends and enemies) the sixth house is second, so the Moon and Jupiter are the Sun's friends. Saturn is in eleventh. Counted from the fifth house, the Saturn is in seventh from it. So the Sun and Saturn are enemies. Mars and Venus are in the fourth—counted from fifth it is the twelfth house. So Mars and Venus are Sun's friends. Thus, in the example horoscope, the following would be the table of temporary friendship and enmity.

Chart of Temporary Friendship and Enmity

Planet	Friend	Enemy
Sun	Moon Mars Jupiter, Venus	Mercury, Saturn
Moon	Sun, Mars, Mercury, Venus	Jupiter, Saturn
Mars	Sun, Moon, Mercury, Jupiter	Venus, Saturn
Mercury	Moon, Mars, Jupiter, Venus	Sun, Saturn
Jupiter	Sun, Mars Mercury, Venus	Moon, Saturn
Venus	Sun, Moon, Mercury, Jupiter	Mars, Saturn
Saturn		Sun, Moon, Mars, Mercury, Jupiter, Venus

Resultant Relationship

Now, the next step is to determine the resultant relationship. Two kinds of relationship have been given above—natural and temporary. A planet may be a friend in one kind and an enemy in the other or a friend at both the places or an enemy in both kinds of relationship. So there can be several permutations and combinations and the resultant relationship is as follows:

(*i*)   friend at both the places—great friend.
(*ii*) enemy at both the places—great enemy.
(*iii*) friend at one place and an enemy at another—neutral.
(*iv*) neutral in natural relationship and a friend in temporary—friend.
(*v*)   neutral in natural relationship and an enemy in temporary—enemy.

Thus, Mercury is Sun's neutral in natural relationship and an enemy in the temporary one. So Mercury is Sun's enemy. The Moon is a friend at both the places so the Moon is Sun's great friend and so on. Working on this way we make the following table:

Table of Resultant Relationship

Sun:	Great friends: Moon, Mars and Jupiter. Neutral: Venus. Enemy: Mercury. Great enemy: Saturn.
Moon:	Great friends: Moon and Mercury. Friends: Mars and Venus. Enemies: Jupiter and Saturn.
Mars:	Great friends: Sun, Moon and Jupiter. Neutral: Mercury. Enemies : Venus and Saturn.
Mercury:	Great friends: Venus. Friends: Mars and Jupiter. Neutrals: Sun and Moon. Enemy: Saturn.
Jupiter:	Great friends: Sun and Mars. Neutrals: Moon, Mercury and Venus. Enemy: Saturn.
Venus:	Great friend: Mercury. Friend: Jupiter. Neutrals: Sun, Moon and Saturn. Enemy: Mars.
Saturn:	Enemy: Jupiter. Neutrals: Mercury and Venus. Great enemies: Sun, Moon and Mars.

Why have we dealt with this long process of determining the great friendship, friendship, neutrality, enmity or great enmity between planets? Because, that is to appraise the effects of a planet.

Planets in great friend's sign shed a part of their bad effect and are more inclined to do good. Planets in friend's sign also play the above role but in lesser measure. Planets in neutral's sign have little power to do marked good or marked evil. Planets in enemy's sign lose much of their beneficence and if malefics are more inclined to do evil. Planets in great enemy's sign lose in very great measure their capacity to do good and their propensity to do harm is much increased.

The above applies not only to sign positions but to the *navansha* positions also. If a planet is in, say a great friend's sign, but in a great enemy's *navansha*, then its power to do good would (due to sign position) be curtailed on account of its unfavourable position in *navansha;* and *viceversa.*

It is, however, emphasised that the location in a friend's or enemy's sign or *navansha* is one of the criteria to judge the favourable or unfavourable effects generated by it. There are other criteria also—including some exceptions to the above rule, which we shall deal with in subsequent chapters.

As Rahu and Ketu primarily show the effects of the house they occupy and the planets they are conjoined with, these two shadowy planets have not been dealt with in the context of friendship and enmity between planets.

Benefic and Malefic

(i)   The Sun, Mars, Saturn, Rahu and Ketu are malefic. A malefic planet spoils the good effects of the house it tenants, it also damages the prospects of the house it aspects. This is generally so and particularly during its period and sub-periods (*vide* chapter IX). But there is one exception to it. A malefic if it occupies its own house or aspects its own house—it promotes its good effect and does not spoil it. Which house or houses are aspected by a particular planet has been explained in a subsequent para.

(ii) The Moon, Mercury, Jupiter and Venus are benefic planets. But the Moon on the 14th of the dark-fortnight of the month and on *amavasya* when the Moon conjoins the Sun is not considered a benefic. He is rather considered a malefic. According to some astrologers if Mercury is not conjoined with a benefic but with a malefic instead, he becomes a malefic. A benefic tenanting or aspecting a house generally promotes the good effects of the house tenanted or aspected by it and particularly during its period and sub-periods.

Aspects

Now we shall deal with the aspects of planets.

(*i*)　The Sun, the Moon, Mercury and Venus have full aspect on the seventh houses; 75% on the fourth and the eighth houses 50% on the fifth and the ninth houses and 25% on the third and the tenth houses, as counted from the house (sign) occupied by him in the birth chart.

(*ii*)　Mars fully aspects the fourth, seventh and the eighth houses; his aspect on the fifth and the ninth houses is 50% while on the third and the tenth houses it is only 25%.

(*iii*)　Jupiter has full aspect on the fifth, seventh and ninth houses; on the fourth and the eighth houses it is 75% and on the third and the tenth houses it is 25% only.

(*iv*)　Saturn's aspect on the third, seventh and the tenth houses is full; on the fourth and the eighth houses it is 75% and on the fifth and the ninth 50%.

While counting the houses, we should begin with the house tenanted by the planet whose aspect we are computing. We shall clarify it further by computing the aspects of the Sun in the example horoscope given on (page 22).

Thus, when computing the aspects of the Sun, in the example chart we have to count from the houses occupied by the Sun. The Sun is in the fifth house. So the twelve houses counted from the Sun will be the following houses as counted from the ascendant:

(*i*) 5th, (*ii*) 6th, (*iii*) 7th, (*iv*) 8th, (*v*) 9th, (*vi*) 10th, (*vii*) 11th, (*viii*) 12th, (*ix*) 1st, (*x*) 2nd, (*xi*) 3rd, (*xii*) 4th.

Thus, the seventh house counted from the Sun will be the 11th house from the ascendant. On this house the Sun's aspect would be full. The fourth and the eighth houses counted from the Sun will be the 8th and 12th houses respectively from the ascendant—and on these two houses, the Sun's aspect will be 75%. The fifth and the ninth houses from the Sun will be the 9th and 1st houses respectively from the ascendant and on these houses the Sun's aspect will be 50%. The third and the tenth houses, as counted from the Sun will be the 7th and the 2nd houses respectively from the ascendant. And on these two houses, the Sun's aspect will be 25%.

Another principle, the readers would do well to note is that the planets not only aspect the house but also the planets posited therein. In the example horoscope the Sun is in Scorpio. He has full aspect on Taurus because Taurus is seventh from Scorpio. So the Sun aspects not only Taurus but Saturn also, who occupies that sign in the example chart. Similarly, Saturn in Taurus not only aspects Scorpio but also the Sun and Mercury occupying Scorpio.

It is essential to know and remember this feature of planetary aspects. It is important to remember it for two reasons:

(*i*) Firstly, a benefic aspecting a malefic, reduces the malignance of the aspected planet. Conversely, a malefic aspecting a benefic reduces the benificence of the aspected planet.

(*ii*) Secondly, when two planets fully aspect each other they develop a special connection, bringing about a particular kind of fusion of their influences. This special connection is called *sambandha* in Sanskrit. This is very useful expression, as we would have occasion to refer to it frequently. At a subsequent stage we have explained this term in further detail.

Direction

The following are the directions of the planets:

Direction	Planets	Direction	Planets
East	Sun	West	Saturn
South East	Venus	North West	Moon
South	Mars	North	Mercury
South West	Rahu	North East	Jupiter

If a planet is strong and well placed in a chart it shows gain or benefit from its direction. Conversely, if a planet is weak and afflicted in a birth chart, there may be loss or trouble in the particular direction.

Colours, Jewels and Metals

Below are being given the colours, jewels and metals falling in the portfolio of each planet:

(*i*)   Sun: copper colour, ruby, copper.

(*ii*)   Moon: white, pearl, silver.

(*iii*)   Mars: red coral, copper and gold.

(*iv*)   Mercury: green, emerald, gold, also alloy of metals.

(*v*)   Jupiter: yellow, yellow sapphire, gold.

(*vi*)   Venus: of variegated colour, also white, diamond, silver.

(*vii*)   Saturn: black, blue sapphire, iron.

(*viii*)   Rahu: dark, *gomed* (this is a Sanskrit word and the jewel is known by this name. It is like garnet in appearance but different from it), lead and gold.

(*ix*)   Ketu: spotted colour, cat's eye, gold and alloy of metals.

If a planet is strong in the nativity dealing in metals, jewels or commodities conforming to its colour is beneficial. If a planet is weak, the metal and jewel pertaining to the planet should be worn next to the skin to mitigate its evil effects. For further details please see Chapter X.

The colour of the planet also helps in determining the complexion. Planets in the first house (the ascendant) bestow their respective complexions to the native. For example, the Moon, Jupiter or Venus in the first house would make the native fair; Saturn or Rahu therein would make him dark. As we judge wife in a male nativity and husband in a female nativity from the seventh house, planets in the seventh house and aspecting it would determine the complexion of the wife or the husband as the case may be. If no planet is there, then we judge from the planets aspecting the seventh house and the planet, who is the lord of the seventh.

Sex

All the planets are males. In western astrology the Moon and Venus are referred to as she and the other planets as he. But in Hindu astrology all the planets are referred to as he. There is a mythological tale that the Moon had liaison with Jupiter's wife

Tara and she gave birth to Mercury from this union. Yet another such story has it that Venus (also called *Ushanas* in Sanskrit) had two wives *Jayanti* (daughter of *Indra*) and *Go* (daughter of *Pitri*) and he had four sons *Twashtra, Varutrin, Shanda* and *Marka*. Thus, all the nine planets (including Rahu and Ketu which are merely sensitive Points) are referred to as he. But in endowing influence, the Sun, Mars and Jupiter are treated as males, the Moon and Venus as females, Mercury as a male eunuch and Saturn as a female eunuch. These qualities are made use of in determining the sex of children by taking into consideration, the lord of the fifth house (from which we judge children) and the planets tenanting and aspecting the fifth house. The eunuch planets give more daughters than sons.

Ingredients of Body

If a planet is strong in the birth chart, the corresponding ingredient would be strong in the body and *vice versa*. Planets which are weak and afflicted in a chart cause ailments and diseases pertaining to the ingredient over which they preside. The relationship between the planets and the ingredients of the body is as follows:

(*i*) Sun—bones, (*ii*) Moon—blood, (*iii*) Mars—marrow, (*iv*) Mercury—skin, (*v*) Jupiter—fat, (*vi*) Venus—semen in males and ovaries in females, (*vii*) Saturn—the nerves.

The diagnosis of diseases according to the Hindu system of medicine is on the basis of imbalance of one, two or all the three humours called *vata* (wind), *pitta* (bile) and *kapha* (phlegm).

The relationship between the planets and the three humours is as follows:

(*i*) Sun—bile, (*ii*) Moon—wind and phlegm, (*iii*) Mars—bile, (*iv*) Mercury, wind, bile and phlegm, (*v*) Jupiter—phlegm (*vi*) Venus—wind and phlegm, (*vii*) Saturn—wind.

Taste

Below are being given the tastes or flavours pertaining to each planet. The second house in a birth chart represents the mouth and the tongue. The native is fond of dishes of a particular taste or flavour governed by the planet tenanting or aspecting the second house:

(*i*) Sun—bitter, (*ii*) Moon—saline, (*iii*) Mars—pungent, (*iv*) Mercury—mixture of various flavours, (*v*) Jupiter—sweet, (*vi*) Venus—sour, (*vii*) Saturn—astringent.

When the time of birth in not exact and there is a chance of one of the two consecutive signs rising, use of this prognostication is made to identify the ascendant, by taking into account as to which planet or planets fall in the second house or aspect it.

Directional Strength

Mercury and Jupiter are strong in the first house, the Moon and Venus in the fourth, Saturn in the seventh and the Sun and Mars in the tenth. These are the houses where they are strong. In the respective seventh houses from the above, they are the weakest. Thus, Mercury and Jupiter will be weak in the seventh (from the ascendant); the Moon and Venus would be weak in the tenth from the ascendant, Saturn in the first and the Sun and Mars in the fourth. In between, their strength should be calculated by rule of three.

We have stated in an earlier chapter as to which particular matter of department or life is to be judged from which house. But there is a parallel line of judgment. Each planet stands for certain matters and in Judging that particular matter not only the house (from which that matter is judged) the house lord. Planets tenanting or aspecting the particular house are taken into consideration but also the particular planet, called *Karaka* (significator) who has a special connection with the specific matter under consideration. We shall explain the point further, but let us first enumerate the various matters which fall in the port folio of each planet.

(*i*) The Sun represents the soul; the Moon the heart (the physical organ heart, as well as the representative emotions); Mars the stamina and prowess; Mercury speech and intelligence; Jupiter happiness, learning and wisdom, Venus worldly comforts, enjoyment in life (the pleasures

of sex being one of these) and conveyances; Saturn
hard work and sorrow.

(*ii*) The Sun stands for father, the Moon for mother, Mars for
brothers and sisters, Mercury for maternal uncle, Jupiter
for sons and daughters (according to some astrologers in
female nativities, Jupiter stands for husband also). Venus
for wife/husband, and Saturn for servants.

(*iii*) While judging matters pertaining to the first house, also
take note of the Sun. In the judgment of the second, fifth
and eleventh houses also take into consideration how
Jupiter is placed in the chart while judging the third
house take cognisance of Mars as well. In matters
pertaining to the fourth house do not fail to take into
consideration how the Moon and Mercury are disposed.
While appraising the sixth house, due consideration
should be bestowed on Mars and Saturn also. In the
judgment of the seventh house equal weight should be
attached to Venus, while examining the eighth and the
twelfth houses attach due importance to Saturn as well.
While judging the ninth house take into consideration if
the Sun and Jupiter are well-placed and strong or weak
and afflicted. In the judgment of the tenth house apart
from the house and its lord, take cognisance of the Sun,
Mercury, Jupiter and Saturn as well.

We shall further clarify the above, so that, those who are
new to the study of astrology may well understand and
appreciate the import of the above dicta. For example, we judge
the body and the vigour, the health and general
capability of the native from, the first house. Now suppose the
first house is strong which implies that its lord is strong, well-
placed and well-aspected and benefics tenant and/or aspect
the first house then the native will have good health. But, if
despite the above features being present, the Sun in the chart
is weak, ill-placed and afflicted, the health may not be so good.
Or take another example. We judge the mother from the fourth
house and the Moon. If the fourth house is strong but the Moon

weak, ill-placed and afflicted the native may not have full happiness in respect of the mother.

Combust Planets

When a planet due to nearness to the Sun, has its (Planet's) rays burnt up or damaged, it is called combust. A combust planet is considered weak and afflicted.

When the Moon is behind the Sun and is at a distance of 24 degrees from the Sun up to the time he conjoins the Sun, he is considered very weak. Since mercury and Venus are always near the Sun, (Mercury is never more than 28 degrees away from the Sun and Venus never more than 48 degrees from the Sun) the combustion of Mercury and Venus is not considered so evil. But Jupiter if combust fails to give its full good effect. Mars and Saturn, when combust, if beneficial in the particular chart under consideration, do not show full good effect, but if they are malignantly disposed in the chart, then the phenomenon of combustion makes them still more malignant. The ephemeris for the year of the birth must be looked up to ascertain if any planet was combust on the date of birth.

When a planet is combust, it cannot be seen in the sky. When it is not combust it is visible at night.

CHAPTER VI

PLANETS IN SIGNS

We have discussed in the preceding chapter the relative merits of planets occupying great friend's, friend's, neutral's, enemy's and great enemy's sign. Now, we shall examine in detail the effects of planets occupying various signs.

If a planet on other counts is expected to show good results, it does so in a marked measure, when it is in its sign of exaltation, or in its own sign. To this must be added two provisos. If a planet is a malefic and occupies sign of exaltation, it shows very good results in respect of the house or houses of which it is the lord, but spoils in some measure the house it occupies or aspects. This is in regard to malefics. As regards the benefics, if they are in exaltation they do good both to the house or houses they are lords of and also to the house they occupy or aspect.

A planet in its own sign is deemed to do good in respect of the house it owns and occupies and also in regard to the affairs of the other house, if it is the lord of two houses. But there is an exception to the above rule. Second house governs accumulated wealth but the lord of the second house, at the appropriate age causes death also. Similarly, the seventh house governs conjugal happiness, but the lord of the seventh house is also capable of causing death.

The twelfth house governs expenses. Now if the lord of the second is in second, this would lead to accumulation of wealth, but the lord of the second (due to ownership of a fatal house called *maraka* in Sanskrit) on account of occupying the second also becomes a greater *maraka*. (This word in Sanskrit means a killer and is a frequently occurring astrological nomenclature which readers would do well to remember). Similarly, if the lord of the seventh is in seventh, it is a good prognostication for conjugal happiness, but the planet acquires more *maraka* (killing) propensities due to its occupying the seventh house. When the lord of the twelfth is in twelfth the native will be prone to incur heavy expenses, particularly so, if the planet is a malefic one. Barring these special features, it is always beneficial to have the planet in its own sign. If a planet, on various counts (which we shall discuss in subsequent chapters) is inclined to do good, it will do so if it tenants its great friend's sign, the efficacy to do good is in lesser measure if it is in its friend's sign and is still less if it is in its neutral's sign. If it is in its enemy's sign the efficacy is much curtailed and it is least if in its great enemy's sign.

Conversely, if a planet is on various counts, (as discussed hereafter) inclined to do evil, the consequences are not so detrimental if it is in its friend's sign and still less if in its great friends sign. In a neutral's sign, the evil propensity is normal but in an enemy's sign it is much enhanced and the evil is maximum if the planet is in its great enemy's sign.

A debilitated planet is deemed very weak and is capable of doing very little good to the house or house it owns. If the debilitated planet be a malefic one, it spoils very much the house it tenants and aspects but if it be a benefic one, it does not spoil the house it occupies or aspects. The exception to this general rule is that debilitated Jupiter in the seventh house is not considered good for the longevity of the wife.

While discussing the debilitated planets, we have to invite attention to one special dictum by Mantreshwar an eminent astrologer who flourished in the sixteenth century. He states:

"When a planet is retrograde, it produces effects as if it were in its sign of exaltation, though it be in debilitation or in its enemy's sign. Similarly a planet in *vargottam* shows the effect as if it were in its own sign." (*Phala Deepika*, Chapter IX, Verse 20).

Certain other circumstances, also mitigate the evil influence of debilitated planets.

(*i*) If the debilitated planet conjoins with an exalted planet (for example Mars and Jupiter both together in Cancer where Mars would be debilitated and Jupiter exalted) the evil effects of the debilitated planet are mitigated, but as consequence of conjunction the good effects of the exalted planet are also curtailed.

(ii) If the lord of the sign occupied by a debilitated planet fully aspects the debilitated planet, the evil is in some measure mitigated,

Having explained the general rules for assessing a planet in the various signs, we are giving below what Varah Mihir, an eminent astronomer and astrologer of India, who flourished two thousand years ago, has stated in regard to sign positions. The following descriptions have been taken from Chapter XVI of his *Hora Shastra.*

The Ascendant or the Moon

In Hindu astrology the moon sign is attached the same value as the rising sign (the ascendant). If the ascendant or the Moon is in—

Aries: Round eyes with pinkish tint, the native is fond of hot food and vegetables and eats quickly; is fond of roaming (walking) and going about places; is easily contented; is more than normally sexed; is fond of women; money does not accumulate with him; his tastes are variable; proud and very active; clever in fighting; has bad nails; afraid of water; is generally the eldest among his brothers and sisters.

Taurus: Has large face and thighs; has a playful gait; has mole or some mark on the face or the back; generous in giving; has more daughters than sons; has more of phlegm in his body; leaves off his earlier relations and lives with newly formed ones; has much appetite, is of a forgiving nature; has permanent friends; the middle and last portions of life are happier than the earlier one.

Gemini: Has black eyes; a prominent nose; curly hair and a pleasing appearance; very amorous with women and of a flirting disposition; learned; acts well as a messenger or a middle man;

very intelligent; has sweet speech; humorous; can fathom the desires of others; good at gambling; pleasing appearance; fond of music and songs; well-versed in the art of dancing; a glutton; has friendship with eunuchs.

Cancer: Not tall; has a thick neck; walks quickly and in a slightly curved direction; is at times very rich, at others has no money—thus in matters of wealth, he is waxing and waning like the Moon; is fond of and inclined to do good to his friends; fond of astrology and of water reservoirs and gardens; is under the influence of wife/women; has good friends, owns houses ; is amenable to reason and good counsel.

Leo: Large face and prominent chin; pale yellowish eyes; suffers from diseases arising out of hunger and thirst, also from diseases of the stomach, mental and dental ailments; generous in giving; of a fixed temperament; proud and chivalrous; fiery in temper and takes offence even at trifles; has a few sons; does not have very harmonious relations with wife/women; is doted upon by his mother.

Virgo: Beautiful eyes, with shy and languid glances; loose arms and shoulders; intelligent; learned; religious and clever in arts and crafts; of sweet speech; amiable in manners and devoted to truth; overfond of sex; happy; benefits from other people's wealth and property; lives at a place other than his homeland, has few children—mostly daughters.

Libra: Tall, lean and thin; has a prominent nose; liable to become frequently indisposed; may have some infirmity in a limb; intelligent; clean; clever in purchase and sale; wealthy; does good to his relations, but he is displeased with him and they forsake him; is devoted to gods, *brahmans* and ascetics; is under the influence of his wife/women; may have two names— one associated with gods.

Scorpio: Large eyes; broad chest; round thighs, knees and calves of legs; of pale yellow complexion; suffers ill-health during childhood; premature separation from father or religious preceptor; is cruelly inclined in thoughts and actions; secretly indulges in many sinful acts; is respected by the king and the government.

Sagittarius: Very large face and neck; thick teeth, and big lower lip; big ears and nose; fleshy arms; stooping shoulders; bad nails; eloquent in speech; intelligent; well-versed in arts and crafts; powerful and very clever; bustling with activity; is inimical to relations; inherits father's wealth; generous in giving; cannot be controlled by force but by gentle persuasion only.

Capricorn: Beautiful eyes; lower half of the body not as well-developed as the upper half; thin waist; indolent but endowed with good fortune; cannot bear intense cold; fond of roaming (walking) and going about places; has much stamina; accepts advice of others; though not so religious yet makes much show of religiosity; always doting upon his wife and children; devoid of shame; merciless and avaricious; has liaison with a grown up women related to the native.

Aquarius: Large body with stiff hair all over; neck like that of camel; large face, hands, feet, back,thighs and waist, indulges in sinful acts in relation to other women; not very intelligent; has much fortitude to put up with strenuous labour; fond of flowers and fragrant anointing; firmly attached to friends.

Pisces: Well proportionate body; large head; prominent nose; has beautiful eyes; attached to wife; fond of good apparel; is under the influence of his wife/women; gains from aqueous products; imports and exports; overcomes his enemies; gains from underground wealth. The native is intelligent and learned.

While judging female nativities, she should be substituted for he in the above description and also interpretations altered, *mutatis mutandis,* for certain descriptions—like hairy body may not apply to females and the astrologer is expected to use common sense and discretion which is the life-breath of astrological interpretation.

The Sun

If the Sun is in Aries, the native is famous, clever, fond of roaming but not rich. He may succeed well in a career where he has to bear arms or where he has to trade in arms and ammunitions. In Taurus the native may earn well by trading in cloth and articles having fragrant odour. He is a connoisseur of music and singing, but does not love women well. When the Sun is in Gemini, the native is learned, is fond of astrology and is rich. In Cancer he has little forbearance for perseverance, works quickly but in not able to accumulate much wealth; he is engaged in the employment of others and has to bear much physical strain and mental anguish. If the Sun is in Leo, he is fond of forests, mountains and places where herds of cattle are kept; he has much stamina and is intelligent and valorous. In Virgo, the native has a delicate and attractive body resembling that of a female; he is learned, a good mathematician and well-versed in art, literature, poetry and calligraphy or painting.

When the Sun is in Libra, the native may do well in professions connected with liquors; he is fond of travelling; may resort to low actions for obtaining wealth. In Scorpio the native is cruel, daring and chivalrous; he is very learned and may earn well in professions connected with commodities in which poison is an ingredient. When the Sun is in Sagittarius, the native is sharp (in action and temper); he commands a respect of good society. In Capricorn he is not a good tradesman or deals in articles of inferior value is greedy and inclined to obtain others' money by any means—fair or foul. He is not learned and his industry brings fortune to others. When the Sun is in Aquarius, the native is low-minded, devoid of full happiness in respect of sons and good fortune, he is not wealthy. In Pisces, the native may obtain wealth by dealing in matters and commodities connected with water (shipping, aqueous products, import, export, grain cultivated in watery lands, such as paddy, etc.). He is respected by ladies.

Mars

If Mars is in Aries or Scorpio, the native is respected by the king or the government; he is fond of travelling, a good tradesman and is wealthy. He may have some wounds inflicted on the body and may be the head of a section of an army or some institution. He would be sensuous and much inclined to the pleasures of the flesh. If Mars is in Taurus or Libra, the native is under too much influence of young ladies and has liaison with other people's wives. He is inimically disposed towards his friends. The native is a coward at heart but bullying in speech. He is very cunning and disguises his true intentions. He is fond of dressing well.

If Mars is in Gemini or Virgo, the native is fearless and courageous. He has sons and is wealthy but devoid of friends. He is grateful to persons who do him good. He is well-versed in music and singing as well as in the art of warfare. He solicits favours from others but is himself miserly. If the planet is in Cancer, the native is wealthy and may earn from transport by water. He is learned but suffers from infirmity of (or disease in) some limb and is wicked.

If Mars is in Leo, the native is fearless and fond of roaming in forests. He is capable of bearing much physical hardship, but is devoid of wealth and happiness in respect of wife and sons. If the planet is in Sagittarius or Pisces, he occupies an eminent position. He has plenty of courage and is famous. He has a few sons and a host of enemies. If mars is in Aquarius the native doesn't have riches; he is fond of travelling, is cruel and resorts to untruth. He suffers much mental distress. If the planet is in Capricorn, he has a number of sons and plenty of wealth. He occupies a kingly position.

Mercury

If Mercury is in Aries or Scorpio, the native has little belief in God; he has thievish instincts (*i.e.*, inclined to make money by illegal means) but is not wealthy. He is fond of eating, drinking and gambling. He is attached to an unworthy woman (may be his own wife or some other woman) and his conduct is hypocritical. But if the planet is in Taurus or Libra, the native is respectful to his elders (religious preceptor, parents etc). He is generous in giving, and always engaged in acquisition of wealth. He is lucky in respect of wife/wives and has a number of sons. He is good lecturer, teacher and a public speaker.

If Mercury is in Gemini, he indulges in much self-praise and is garrulous; he is learned and well versed in arts. He speaks in an endearing manner and leads a comfortable life. If the planet is in Cancer, the native earns money from aqueous products, water transport, import, export etc. He is inimical to his own people. If Mercury is in Leo, the native is fond of travelling; he is not much liked by women, suffers in respect of happiness, wealth and sons; he is not learned; is very covetous of women (*i.e.*, has a flirting tendency); he is humiliated by his own people. But if Mercury is in Virgo, the native has a host of good qualities, he is of a forgiving disposition; he is fearless, generous and leads a happy and comfortable life; he has a logical mind and can argue well.

If Mercury is in Sagittarius, he is a favourite of the king (*i.e.*, much liked by his superior authorities).

He is learned and his statements are well thought out and authoritative. If the planet is in Pisces, he excels all his co-workers in rendering meritorious services to his master. He has the art of winning over others. He is good in crafts not requiring much dexterity or skill. If Mercury is in Capricorn or Aquarius he runs errands for others (*i.e.*, occupies a subordinate position) and carries out his duties well; he has to endure much physical hardship, is not rich and remains in debts. He is good in mechanics and crafts.

Jupiter

If Jupiter is in Aries or Scorpio, the native leads a section of an army or occupies an equally eminent position. He is very wealthy, is lucky in respect of wife/wives, and has a number of sons. He is of forgiving disposition, generous and chivalrous and has a host of good qualities. He has good servants. If the planet is in Taurus or Libra, the native has a good body and is healthy; he has friends, riches and sons. He is much liked by people and leads a happy life. He is generous in giving.

If Jupiter is in Gemini or Virgo, the native has paraphernalia of luxury, sons and friends. He may be engaged in giving good counsel to others or in work involving assistance to a man of position.

If the planet is in Cancer, the native has wealth and jewellery, sons and wives[1]. He is intelligent and wise and leads a comfortable life. When Jupiter is in Leo, he is the head of a section of an army or occupies an equally high rank. The other effects for Jupiter in Leo are the same as those described for Jupiter in Cancer.

If Jupiter is in Sagittarius or Pisces, he may be a chieftain or a minister to a king or a commander-in-chief or holds any other high office. He is rich. For Jupiter in Aquarius the same effects should be described as for Jupiter in Cancer. But when the planet is in Capricorn, the native has not much money and does not lead a happy life. He is given to low acts.

Venus

When Venus is in Aries or Scorpio, the native is attached to other peoples' wives and loses his wealth on account of them (directly, by extravagant expenditure on such women or indirectly by taking their side and entering into strife and thereby damaging his own interests). He brings bad name to his family. When the Planet is in Taurus or Libra, the native is fearless, earns much wealth due to his own courage and initiative. He is much favoured by the king (the government). He becomes famous and heads his people.

When Venus is in Gemini, he engages in the service of the government and is well up in arts and crafts. He is wealthy. But when this planet is in Virgo, he resorts to low acts, has to put up with a life of hardships and is not rich.

When Venus is in Cancer, the native has two wives (or may have one wife and one mistress); he is timid. He solicits favours from others. He is vain and suffers much mental distress. If the planet is in Leo, he marries a lady of high family; gains money from/through women but the number of sons is limited. When the planet is in Sagittarius, the native is wealthy and he is respected by clans, groups of people and society. When the

---

1. In ancient India, when this work *Horashastra* (from which excerpts have been given here) was written, rich men frequently had more than one wife.

planet is in Pisces, he has a very pleasing personality, is honoured by the government, is learned and has riches.

When Venus is in Capricorn or Aquarius, the native has a pleasing personality; he is under the dominance of women and attached to an unworthy woman.

Saturn

If Saturn is in Aries the native is not wise, he wanders unnecessarily (*i.e.,* his going about is not fruitful); is devoid of sincere friends; is a hypocrite and deceitful. If the planet is in Scorpio, he may be a victim of physical assault (or accidents) and has to put up with much physical hardship; he is very active but cruel. When Saturn is in Gemini or Virgo, he has not much wealth or happiness, also not much happiness in respect of sons. He engages in the service of a high ranking person (such as government); may be custodian of men or property. He makes frequent slips in writing. He is devoid of shame.

When Saturn is in Taurus, the native is very endearing to prohibited women (with whom one should not have liasion due to close family relationship or due to their profligate character); he has not wealth but has several wives (or love affairs). But when Saturn is in Libra he occupies a very eminent position and is respected by people of the towns/ cities, clans and assemblages of people. He is wealthy and famous. When Saturn is in Cancer, the native's mother may not have her full span of life; the native is not wise; suffers in respect of sons , his teeth are set apart. When the planet is in Leo, the native's conduct is low, he does not have a happy life; he has not much happiness in respect of sons either; he has to lead a life of drudgery.

When Saturn is in Sagittarius or Pisces, the native is more happy and prosperous in the last one third part of life; he wins the confidence of high authorities; has a good wife and sons. He may by leader of men or occupy a high Position. He has riches. When Saturn is in Capricorn or Aquarious the native has the enjoyment of other peoples' wives and riches. His prosperity is abiding. He earns much but also spends freely on his comforts;

he is not of clean habits and his eyes may not be strong.

Rahu and Ketu

It is good for Rahu to be in Aries, Taurus, Gemini, Cancer, Virgo or Capricorn. Naturally, Ketu will be in the seventh from Rahu because they are always 180° apart—so if Rahu is in Aries, Ketu would be in Libra and so on.

CHAPTER VII

PLANETS IN HOUSES

Now, we shall deal with the effects of individual planets in the twelve houses. Before we proceed to delineate these, the readers are requested to understand well the difference between a sign and a house. As stated earlier, for one month, the Sun is generally in one sign travelling from the first degree to the 30th degree—travelling at the rate of about one degree per day. But the house position of the Sun would be different after every two hours—because in twenty-four houses he will have passed through all the twelve houses.

We have given in the previous chapter characteristic for persons, according to the sign rising, and also according to the location of the planets in various signs. We are also giving, hereunder, the effects of planets in houses. But these effects are however modified due to conjunction with and aspects of other planets. We shall clarify the point.

Suppose we find the Moon in Virgo in a birth chart. Now if this Moon is conjoined with or aspected by Jupiter, the quality of the Moon's effects would be much improved because Jupiter is a first rate benefic. On the other hand, if instead of Jupiter, Saturn aspects the Moon, as Saturn is a first rate malefic, his aspect would depress the good qualities of the Moon. And what applies to aspects, holds good for conjunctions also.

While judging the effects of the rising sign or the Moon in a particular sign, due regard should be paid to the lord of the sign (the rising sign or the sign in which the Moon is). Suppose the rising sign is Sagittarius. Now, Jupiter is the lord of Sagittarius. So if Jupiter is strong by sign say in Pisces (in his own sign) conjoined with a benefic and aspected by a benefic, the good effects described for Sagittarius (as rising sign or moonsign) would be much enhanced. But if on the contrary say Jupiter is debilitated in Capricorn, conjoined with a malefic and aspected by a malefic, the good effects would be much devalued.

The art of astrological interpretation comprises blending of influences and synthesising at times even the contrary ones. If a planet at birth is expected to show good results on one count and an evil one on another count—they are set off and the resultant influence (or balance, if it is good or otherwise) prevails. This rule is in regard to the diverse or contrary influences of the one and the same planet. But even here if the influences pertain to different departments of life both would be operative. Suppose Taurus is the sign rising, and Mars and Saturn are together in Virgo in the fifth house. Now a combination of the lords of the seventh, ninth and tenth houses would be good for wealth and position but evil for fifth house affairs (stomach, children) due to malefic being in the fifth.

Those who are not well-acquainted with the principle of astrology may raise their eye-brows and exclaim "how can one and the same planet be good as well as bad at the same time. Either he should be good or he should be bad !" But this argument does not hold good in astrology. A planet may be good on account of lordship (*i.e.,* by being lord of good houses) but evil due to sign or house position. When judging a planet we have to take into account his lordship, sign position, the location in a house, conjunction with and aspects from other planets etc.

To revert to the main point under discussion when two planets indicate two contrary influences—say Jupiter in the birth chart indicates wealth and Saturn prognosticates poverty— the two contrary influences are not set off. When there is time for Jupiter's influence to operate—there will be wealth and when Saturn's influence would be current, wealth would be drained off and there would be poverty[1]

---

1. See Rudra's Commentary *Vivarana* pages 185 and 186 published by Kerala University.

The method to determine when a particular planet's influence would be operative in the life of the person whose birth chart is under consideration has been explained in Chapter X. With these preliminary guide lines for judging the effects of planets, we are giving below the effects of planets in the twelve houses.

First House

Sun: The native is fearless, cruel and firm in his resolve, but his eye-sight suffers, But if the Sun is in Aries, he is very rich and famous, If the Sun is in Leo, he gets night-blindness (in old age); if in Cancer there may be some speck in the eye; if in Libra, the native is devoid of wealth and vision fails (in old age). According to *Jataka Parijata* if the Sun is in the first house, the number of sons is limited, the native is hard-hearted but leads a comfortable life; he eats little and suffers from eyediseases. He is boastful but well-bred in manners. If the Sun is in Pisces, the native has much stamina and has good company of damsels; the eye-sight suffers. According to *Phala deepika*, the Sun in the first house inclines to boldness.

Moon: If waning Moon on the 14th and the 15th of the dark fortnight occupies the first house, the native suffers form some defective limb or is deaf and dull; if such a Moon be conjoined with a malefic he does not live long and works in an inferior position. But if the Moon be full the native is learned and long-lived. The Moon in Aries. Taurus or Cancer gives a pleasing personality, wealth and good name and fame.

Mars: The native is courageous, cruel, very active and fond of travelling, his health is not so good. He may get hurt in the head. Even in old age he appears young. Mars gives very good results if in Aries, Leo, Scorpio, Sagittarius or Capricorn in the first house.

Mercury: The native is learned, wealthy, religious and virtuous. He is intelligent and active. Mercury herein would particularly show very good results if in Gemini or Virgo.

Jupiter: The native is wise and learned. He is long lived and leads a prosperous life. He has a very pleasing appearance. Jupiter would show very good results if in Cancer, Sagittarius and Pisces.

Venus: The native has a pleasing personality; is very sexy and well-versed in amorous arts, he leads a comfortable life. The native is learned and fortunate in respect of wife and children. Venus herein would show particularly good results if in Taurus, Libra or Pisces.

Saturn: Poor, sickly, hard hearted and cunning having an uncouth appearance, always hankering for sexual pleasure, given to low acts, suffers illness in childhood; does not speak distinctly, has stinking nostrils; even when young he has the appearance of an older man. But if Saturn is in Libra, Sagittarius or Pisces, he has host of good qualities (instead of bad ones described above) and rises very high in life. He is firm, pushing, wise and occupies a kingly position. Even in Capricorn or Aquarius Saturn bestows very good effects. The native rises high in life.

Rahu: The native is cruel, merciless, irreligious and sickly, suffers from some disease in the upper part of the body. But Rahu in Aries, Taurus or Cancer in the first house is considered good for longevity.

Ketu: The native is very avaricious and sickly. He is a back-biter; is ungrateful; does not have much happiness.

Note : If benefics aspect or tenant the first house, the evil effects of the nodes is not felt. They become good.

According to *Jataka parijata*, Rahu in Leo in the first house, gives wealth an luxuries. Ketu in Capricorn or Aquarius in the first, gives sons and abiding wealth.

Second House

Sun: Is liberal in spending; possesses precious metals (wealth); is eloquent in speech; has plenty of wealth, but a part of it is appropriated by the government (by penalty or taxation); suffers from diseases of the mouth or eye unless the Sun is in his own sign.

Moon: Over-fond of sex; has comely body and sweet speech; quick in following the hints of others; affluent and devoted to learning; has a large family.

Mars: Plenty of wealth but heavy expenditure also; disease of the eye, teeth and mouth; fond of travelling; may be engaged in trade or manufacturer of metals and agriculture. The native is short-tempered and is of harsh speech; does not eat wholesome food.

Mercury: Earns money by dint of his intelligence and trading capacity; is well-mannered and a gentleman. He is wealthy.

Jupiter: Very agreeable, sweet speech, eloquent as well as learned; gets good and rich food; very rich but liberal in spending.

Venus: Learned, well up in amorous arts and enjoys life; very rich and his speech is endearing.

Saturn: Is untruthful and has a tendency to deceive others; very active and fond of travelling, but unless Saturn is in his own sign or in exaltation or well aspected the native is not able to accumulate much wealth. There may be diseases of the mouth or eyes and he may have to pay financial penalty to the government.

Rahu: He is quarrelsome, deceptive in speech and a part of his wealth may be lost by theft or due to unwise investment.

Ketu: Uses very foul tongue—he unnecessarily contradicts others and creates enemies due ot his bitter and incisive speech; loss of wealth due to servants or theft.

Third House

Sun: Intelligent and chivalrous; his attendants and subordinates would be wicked. The native is very rich and philanthropic.

Moon: Temperate in thought and deed but has a streak of cruelty; he is very popular among his relations but is only moderately rich.

Mars: Intelligent and valorous; has immense prowess and becomes famous; he may bear arms; his conduct is open and straightforward.

Mercury: Humble (temperamentally or due to lack of wealth) outwardly but wicked at heart; his mind is intent upon deceiving others by hypocrisy. These evil traits of character are however not present if Mercury is in Gemini or Virgo. The native is very active and fond of travelling.

Jupiter: Is miserly yet his wealth is drained off; he is under the influence of wife/women. His conduct is not virtuous.

Venus: His speech is tinged with anger; he is too much under the influence of his consort; his conduct is sinful; miserly in spending. Venus in the third causes sorrow and ill health but Venus does not show evil effects, if he is in advance of the Sun *i.e.,* in a sign which precedes the sign tenanted by the Sun. Under such a circumstance, Venus shows very good results.

Saturn: Eats sparingly; he is wealthy, well-bred and possesses good family traits; is intelligent and chivalrous.

Rahu: Very heroic and rich.

Ketu: Rich and possesses many virtuous qualities.

Fourth House

Sun: Cruel, devoid of wealth and intelligence; suffers mental distress and enjoys little happiness; may suffer from heart disease. These evil effects will not manifest themselves if the Sun is in Leo or Scorpio.

Moon: Is learned and has an amiable disposition; leads a happy and comfortable life but there will be many change of residence in old age; will covet other people's wives.

Mars: Devoid of happiness and suffers much mental distress; has no relations he can depend upon; under the influence of wife/women; very heroic. The evil effects will not be felt if Mars is in Aries. Scorpio or Capricorn.

Mercury: Given to scholarly pursuits; is very rich, but there is not much happiness in respect of relations.

Jupiter: Eloquent in speech; physically strong and has a pleasing personality; is rich and famous; he leads a happy and comfortable life; but his intentions and inclinations are wicked.

Venus: Eloquent in speech, intelligent, learned, leads a happy and rich life but the native is dominated by wife/women.

Saturn: Devoid of happiness; has to suffer much mental anguish; inwardly wicked; tries to deceive others by false pretences; trouble to mother; illness during childhood.

Rahu: Not much happiness; not long lived; Rahu herein causes sorrow unless conjoined with the lord of the fourth, fifth or ninth.

Ketu: Suffers in respect of mother, house, conveyance, landed property and cattle—are destroyed. The evil is mitigated if the lord of the fourth is in fourth or Ketu is conjoined with the lord of the fifth or ninth.

Fifth House

Sun: Impairs the longevity of sons; devoid of wealth; likes to live at a place other than his homeland; not of fixed determination; favoured by the government.

Moon: Is inclined to prayers through religious incantations; rich, benevolent and kind; steady application to resolution; has sons (children).

Mars: There may be illness to or premature death of a child (unless Mars be in his own sign in the fifth) or aspected by benefics; stomach trouble; rich and enjoys life; cruel; fond of travelling; not very religious; very brave and active.

Mercury: Endowed with good name and fame and education; has a good wife and sons; wealthy and strong; clever in achieving his objectives (acquisition of wealth etc. or annihilation of enemy) by incantations or sacred prayers; may become a counsellor or minister or work in advising capacity.

Jupiter: Intelligent; virtuous, having many good qualities and attainments; has paraphernalia of luxuries but has limited number of sons.

Venus: Is of very adorable appearance; has good sons; friends and wealth; commands a host of subordinates and conveyances; leads a comfortable life.

Saturn: Proud, long lived, very active but not happy; is virtuous and religious and overcomes a host of enemies; an unfavourable position for sons and wealth (unless the planet here is in Capricorn or Aquarius).

Rahu: Timid, compassionate and devoid of wealth.

Ketu: The native is sickly—there may be chronic stomach trouble; afraid of water; wicked at heart.

Sixth House

Sun: The native is very proud and heroic, he is wealthy and famous; respected by the king (government); is strong and overcomes his enemies.

Moon: Has a soft body with much protoplasm; the appetite is not strong; the sexual power is weak or moderate; easily gets into temper and is indolent; has many enemies; if the birth is at round about the new Moon, the native would not be long lived, but if the birth be about full Moon, the native is long lived and has much enjoyment in life.

Mars: The native is strong and pushing; annihilates his enemies; good digestive power; is wealthy and has a number of men working under him and becomes well-known.

Mercury: Has no enemies (or overcomes them); fond of learning; follows literary pursuits; does not have amiable manners; likely to be quarrelsome; is little inclined to do good to his relations.

Jupiter: Lustful not very strong but victorious over his enemies or has no enemies at all. But this position is slightly unfavourable for sons, particularly if Leo or Scorpio is in the rising sign.

Venus: Suppresses his enemies; suffers from sorrows; his reputation may be sullied: not a happy position for conjugal happiness, particularly if Aries or Scorpio be the rising sign; may have extra-marital relations.

Saturn: The native is under constant apprehension and trouble from the enemies, though he ultimately triumphs over them; good digestive power; eats much, rich, over-sexed; not agreeable temper.

Rahu: Brings credit to the family; long lived; leads happy and comfortable life; overcomes his opponents.

Ketu: Earns good name; is fond of his relations and obliges them; is learned; has many excellent qualities.

Seventh House

Sun: The native suffers insult and humiliation at the hands of or on account of women. He is of fiery temper and wicked; incurs enmity of women; In female nativities this position gives disagreement with husband, unless the Sun is in his own sign Leo.

Moon: Very lustful (over-sexed) and jealous; under the influence of wife/women; merciful; fond of travelling; has much enjoyment in life.

Mars: Suffers distress on account of wife/women (if other indications confirm), there may be premature separation from consort); is fond of fighting; takes cudgels against opponents.

Mercury: Has good knowledge of religion and sticks to the moral code; well-versed in arts and crafts; mirthful and clever; may suffer from infirmity (or disease) in some limb.

Jupiter: Excels his father (in learning, wealth, position etc.) but is not very obedient to his father or the religious preceptor; patient and persevering; has a good wife.

Venus: Handsome and attractive; intensely sexual and well up in amours; inclined to picking up quarrels; much liked by flirting women; may suffer from infirmity (or disease) in some limb.

Saturn: May have a number of liaison; suffers humiliation at the hands of or on account of women; is put to much physical stress and string leads toilsome life with several persons.

Rahu: Proud; suffers from diseases; inclined to liaison.

Ketu: Not wise; dejected in speech; indolent and sleepy; fond of travelling; not well-bred; wife may be sickly. This is a malefic influence and impairs conjugal happiness.

Eighth House

Sun: Limited number of sons; impaired eye-sight; the native has an endearing personality and has strategic skill in fighting (or arguments); is ever discontented.

Moon: Very intelligent; but suffers from chronic diseases; fond of fighting; liberal in giving; mirthful; follows intellectual pursuits. If the birth be in the dark fortnight and during day[1] or during the bright fortnight, during the night, the child is long-lived, otherwise chances of premature death.

Mars: Limited sons; eye-trouble; overspends and incurs debts; diseases in the anus; dressess unostentatiously; wields authority over a large number of people. According to *Jataka Parijata*,

---

1. Form sunrise to sunset is deemed day; from sunset to sunrise night.

the native is rich but according to our experience, however rich he may be, he runs an overdraft account.

Mercury: Very famous and well-renowned for his good qualities; a leader; the native is rich and courteous.

Jupiter: Given to low acts (not in conformity with the standard of his family); intelligent; has good memory; long-lived.

Venus: Very strong (physically); commands all kinds of luxurious paraphernalia; rich; leads a comfortable life but his actions may not be commendable; unless Venus be in Taurus of Libra the native may suffer from urinary complaints *e.g.,* spermatorrhoea (leucorrhoea in case of women).

Saturn: The number of sons is limited unless Virgo or Libra is the rising sign; eye-sight suffers; wealth and vitality suffer but is long-lived; very chivalrous; his temper is easily aroused.

Rahu: Sickly and dilatory in work; has to put up with much trouble; earns a bad name.

Ketu: Covets other people's wives and money; sickly; very greedy; immoral conduct. But if benefics aspect the eighth house, the native is rich and long-lived.

Ninth House

Sun: Has an inimical attitude towards his father and religious preceptor; follows the tenets of religion other than his own; rich; blessed with sons; leads a happy and comfortable life.

Moon: Devoted to father, manes and gods; has a sacrificing spirit; blessed with sons, friends and relations; the native is rich and fortunate.

Mars: Sinful (his acts may be against the moral code); his attitude to his father will be refractory or there may be premature separation from father; but the native become well renowned.

Mercury: Blessed with wealth and sons; leads a happy and comfortable life; is moral and religious; learned; his conduct is commendable.

Jupiter: Devoted to religious austerities; wise and religious; becomes a minister to a king or occupies an equally eminent position[1].

---

1. *Saravali*—an ancient Sanskrit text on astrology gives detailed effects for Jupiter in the ninth according as he is aspected by one or the other of the planets (see *Saravali*, Chapter 32).

Venus: Endowed with wealth and learning; blessed with good wife and sons; rich ; religious; enjoys luxurious paraphernalia.

Saturn: Wealthy; has sons; leads a comfortable life; more philosophical than religious; famous for his exploits in a battlefield (*i.e.,* a good fighter in his sphere of work) matrimonial happiness is curtailed.

Rahu: Wealthy and famous; not much inclined to follow the religious code; contradicts others in speech; inimical to father.

Ketu: Eloquent; proud and brave; of fiery temperament; not religious; talks ill of others; ostentatious; inimical to father.

Tenth House

Sun: Well-bred and virtuous; learned, brave and strong; inherits parental wealth; rises to an eminent position, leads a happy and comfortable life.

Moon: Heroic and religious; intelligent and rich; well up in arts; is successful in all his projects; enjoys luxurious paraphernalia; much enjoyment in life.

Mars: Very rich and leads a comfortable life, best suited to a career where he has to bear arms or to deal with fire (furnaces), very brave and strikes terror in the heart of his enemies; becomes renowned by his actions. Unless Mars is in Aries, Scorpio or Capricorn, this position of Mars is unfaourable for father.

Mercury: Brave; mirthful; rich; leads a happy and comfortable life; gets renown; learned and diplomatic.

Jupiter: Successful in his undertaking; religious and of good conduct; wealth and much respected; learned.

Venus: Gains money from women or agriculture; the native occupies a superior position and leads a happy and comfortable life.

Saturn: Rich, endowed with paraphernalia of comforts; very bold and proud; a strict disciplinarian; he may occupy a position of authority where he inflicts punishment or penalty on others; brings renown to his family.

Rahu: Aggressive in conduct; lacking in amiable manners; the native would be inclined to make money by unfair means; ever eager to take up cudgels.

Ketu: Fond of travelling; strong and very heroic; popular; opposes others; well up in arts and crafts; is inclined to spiritual knowledge.

Eleventh House

Sun: Very rich; has sons, wife, servants and a comfortable life; gains from government or highly placed people.

Moon: Affluent; gains through common people, ladies and aqueous or white products; gets mental depression and is worried without good cause; well renowned.[1]

Mars: Bold; rich; clever in speech; given to much sexual indulgence.

Mercury: Earns much money and fame due to his learning or trading; very wealthy.

Jupiter: Good income; powerful friends; is intelligent and learned; very rich and renowned.

Venus: Gains money through art, aesthetics, white products, women, articles of fashion, automobile industry, cinema; fond of travelling; is inclined to have liaison with others' wives; leads a comfortable life.

Saturn: Enjoys all kinds of luxuries; gains handsome amount from the government, common—masses, iron, oil, petrol, minerals or agriculture; very rich.

Rahu: A good fighter (in the sphere of his work); learned and rich; gains from open as well as hidden sources (not above board); impairs the power of hearing.

Ketu: Much respected by other people and liked by them; of good actions; presides over people; very illustrious; contented; does not indulge in much enjoyment.

Twelfth House

Sun: Fallen from good conduct; persevering; eye-trouble; heavy expenditure; does not have the patronage of highly placed people; deformity (or disease) in some limb. Fond of travelling; blessed with sons.

---

1. If the birth be during day, then the Sun in the eleventh or if the birth be during night then the Moon in eleventh is a favourable factor for longevity.

Moon: May visit foreign countries and live there for some time; not large hearted; trouble in some part of the body.

Mars: His actions are derogatory; eye and teeth trouble; likely to be accused in a criminal case; indebted; opposes others; not much happiness from wife or sons.

Mercury: Inimical to relations; not intelligent; the conduct is not straightforward.

Jupiter: Fond of travelling; not so religiously inclined (unless the planet is in Cancer, Sagittarius or Pisces): his actions will be bereft of kindness.

Venus: Not much happiness in respect of relations; of wicked disposition; enjoys life; may have several extra-marital relationship.

According to *Saravali*, Chapter 34, verse 70 Mercury, Jupiter or Venus (one or more of these) in the twelfth house unless aspected by Mars make one accumulate wealth. The principle underlying is that benefics in twelfth are good.

Saturn: Devoid of wealth; restless mind; eye-trouble; premature teeth decay; not intelligent; fallen form good conduct.

Rahu: Rich; not agreeable in manners, but inclined to do good; suffers from disease in a limb.

Ketu: Waste of accumulated or inherited wealth; fond of travelling; not virtuous in conduct.

While delineating the effects of planets, it should be borne in mind whether the planet is in own house (own sign); friend's sign; neutral's sign or enemy's sign. The variation in shades of interpretation according to the location in own, friend's sign etc., has been dealt with earlier and is not being repeated. Readers are requested to refer in this regard to page (45-46).

Beginners are warned not to make prediction in regard to liaison or extra-marital relations in female charts. There may be other astrological factors, which nullify the influence indicated by one planet. Besides codes of morality differ from country to country and according to times. In western countries flirtation is a common feature but in orthodox families in India, women have a stricter moral code and it is possible, that even a latent desire may not fructify due to moral discipline.

CHAPTER VIII

JUDGING THE CHART

The individual effects of planets in signs and houses have been delineated. They have to be synthesised, for one planet might indicate poverty while the other point to affluent circumstances. The background of the individual must be always kept in mind. Two children may be born in adjoining rooms in a hospital on the same day and at the same time. Yet their physical features, intellectual attainments and moral inclinations differ; their careers start on different lines and their accomplishments are in different spheres. Why? This is due to difference in their heredity and environment in which they are brought up. With these preliminary remarks. We are providing some guidelines for judging the birth chart.

The reader has to go house by house. Each house represents some part of the body, some relation and some department of life. The general principle is that if a house is strong, matters pertaining to it prosper. Here, an objection and a very relevant one might be raised. The position in life. But we find many instances, where the natives lost their fathers at a very tender age and thus were bereft of all happiness in respect of their fathers but rose to very high positions in life. Or take another example. The second house governs the right eye and also wealth. But the native may be immensely rich yet blind. Or take yet another example. The fifth house governs intelligence, education and children. We know persons who have little intelligence, practically no education but have a number of sons.

We shall discuss these distinctions (variation in effects in regard to matters governed by the same house) at a subsequent stage but first we must take up the general principle that if a house is strong, matters pertaining to it prosper and *vice versa*. The factors which fortify a house are as follows:

(*a*) The lord of the house should be strong (*b*) the house should be strong (*c*) the *karaka* or the significator for the house should be strong. We have at a subsequent stage in this chapter explained as to which planet or planets are *karakas* or significators for each house. The readers are requested to bear in mind this important Sanskrit word *karaka*, for it will recur in subsequent discussions.

Now we shall explain how the (*a*) house lord (*b*) house and (*c*) *karaka* should be examined to judge whether these are strong. Let us take each of these one by one.

Lord of the House

The following factors go to make the lord of the house strong. It goes without saying that if the lord of the house is strong, beneficial effects pertaining to the house would flow. But if the lord of the house is weak or afflicted, the matters pertaining to the house will not prosper well, if the lord of the house is very weak and severely afflicted, even disastrous results, pertaining to the house may be felt.

What do we mean by the lord of the house? It has been explained earlier, yet even at the cost of repetition, we may reiterate that the lord of the house means lord of the sign, which falls in a particular house.

Now in order to have a strong lord of the house, it should fulfil the following conditions:

(*i*)   It should be in his sign of exaltation or own house. Even if he is in his own sign, he would show better results in respect of the house he occupies. We shall clarify it by an example. Suppose Scorpio is the sign rising. Jupiter will be in his own sign whether he is in Sagittarius or Pisces. Now, if he is in either of the two signs—he would be good for the second and the fifth houses (in which Sagittarius and Pisces fall respectively) but if he is in Sagittarius he would be better for the second house and if in Pisces he would be better for the fifth house. The next best position is its placement in great friend's sign. If he is in neutral's sign mathematically he is neither strong nor weak, but we would call him weak. If he is in an enemy's sign, he would show little good, would rather pull down the good effects. If he is in great enemy's sign or debilitated, he is very weak, capable of conferring very little benefit and may cause immense harm.

(*ii*) What has been stated above in regard to the sign position of the planet applies to its *navansha* position also.

(*iii*) In order that what we are stating below may be better understood, we are introducing our readers to a technical word 'dispositor' which is frequently used in astrology. The word 'dispositor' in the astrological context means the lord of the sign in which a planet is. Suppose the Moon is in Pisces, then Jupiter lord of Pisces is Moon's dispositor. Suppose Mars is in 11° Leo; then he is in Cancer *navansha*. The lord of Cancer is the Moon, so the Moon would be the *navansha* dispositor of Mars.

Now in judging a planet's strength if the sign dispositor and *navansha* dispositor are strong they add to the planet's strength, *vice versa*. So along with a planet's position in Sign and *navansha*, we have also to look to their dispositors' strength.

(*iv*) The lord of the house should not occupy a bad house. The sixth, eighth and the twelfth houses are called *trik*. This is a Sanskrit word meaning 'the three evil ones' and by usage in astrological parlance, it means the sixth, eighth and the twelfth houses. These houses have been much condemned in Hindu astrology.

Prashna Marga an ancient treatise on Hindu astrology states: "The sages have declared the sixth, eighth and the twelfth as evil houses. The houses, which tenant the lords of these houses or are aspected by them are impaired. The lords of houses which are conjoined with or aspected by the lord of any of these houses (6, 8 and 12) lose their efficacy. Of these the eighth is the worst"

(Chapter XIV Verse 29). The same principle has been enunciated in *Jatakadesh Marga* Chapter X Verse 34.

We have to take into account the sixth, eighth and twelfth not only from the ascendant but from that house also which is under consideration. It is always commendable for a planet to occupy a house from which it can aspect its house. So, if the planet occupies a house from which it cannot aspect its house, it fails to do justice to its house. For example, suppose Cancer is the rising sign. Then counting from Cancer, Leo..... Pisces would constitute the ninth house. We have been told earlier that Jupiter is the lord of Pisces and Jupiter's aspect on the fifth, seventh and ninth (as counted from the house occupied by him) would be full. So it is preferable to have Jupiter in Cancer, Virgo or Scorpio from where he fully aspects his house (Pisces constituting the ninth house— in this example).

Of the two placements—one counted from the ascendant and the other from the house under consideration, the former should weigh more heavily. If the planet is unfavourably placed from both (*i.e.,* the ascendant and the house under consideration) the evil becomes stronger. There are however, some exceptions to the above—(*i*) It is good to have the (*a*) lord of the sixth in eighth or twelfth, (*b*) lord of the eighth in sixth or twelfth and (*c*) the lord of the twelfth in sixth or eighth. (*ii*) The lord of the 1st, 2nd, 3rd, 4th, 5th, 7th, 9th, 10th, and 11th are deemed well placed if they occupy an angle or a trine or the 11th house. The benefic lords of the above houses except the seventh are also deemed well-placed in the second.

(*v*)   The lord of the house should be conjoined with or aspected by benefics. If the lord of the house is by conjuction or aspect associated with malefics its efficacy is impaired. There is also an exception to it—if a planet is lord of an angle and the other lord of a trine—their conjunction is good—irrespective of one or both of these being malefics. The conjunction of the lord of any house (other than that of the 6th, 8th, or 12th) with the lord of the 1st is also good, irrespective of the consideration whether the lord of 1st is a natural benefic or malefic.

(*vi*) The lord of the house should not be combust. The Sun never becomes combust. But the other planets—when they are so near the Sun that they are not visible, are called combust. A combust planet loses part of its efficacy to do good. If it is a malefic, its malignance is increased. A reference to the ephemeris would show whether any planet was combust at birth.

(*vii*) The lord of the house should not be hemmed in between malefics. Hemmed in means that its immediate neighbours on both sides should not be malefics. Suppose Mars is in 13th degree Leo, Moon in 20th degree Leo and Saturn in 28th degree Leo, then the Moon would be hemmed in by Mars on one side and Saturn on the other would be treated as hemmed in between malefics. But if in the above example suppose there is Jupiter in 15th degree Leo then Moon's immediate neighbour would be Jupiter and Saturn, and the Moon will not be hemmed in between malefics. Take another example. Suppose there is Venus in 13th degree Leo, Moon in 20th degree Leo and Jupiter in 28th degree Leo, then the Moon would be hemmed in between benefics. But if there is a malefic say Saturn in 17th degree Leo then the Moon will not be hemmed in between benefics because Moon's immediate neighbour would be Saturn and Jupiter. Suppose there is Mars in Libra the Sun in Scorpio and Saturn in Sagittarius then also the Sun would be deemed to be hemmed in between malefics because there are malefics in adjoining signs but the effect would not be so acute as when the three planets—the one hemmed in and its two immediate neighbours are in the same sign. When the hemmed in planet is just in the centre of two malefics degreewise (Mars in Libra in 13th degree Sun in 18th degree Scorpio and Saturn in 23rd degree Sagittarius—so that the Sun hemmed in between Mars and Saturn is exactly 35° from

Mars and also 35° from Saturn) the effect is very powerful—for good, if hemmed in between benefics and for evil if hemmed in between malefics.

It is good for a planet to be hemmed in between benefics. It improves the benefic qualities of the planet. Being hemmed in between malefics produces the reverse effect.

House

To judge whether a house is strong, the following factors are taken into consideration:

(*i*)   The house should be tenanted by benefics and should not be occupied by malefics. Which planet should be treated as benefics and which others as malefics ? In judging this two factors are taken into consideration: (*a*) the Moon (with 5 digits or more), Mercury, Jupiter and Venus are benefics; Mars, Saturn, Rahu and Ketu are malefics; (*b*) the owners of the 6th, 8th and 12th houses are evil while lords of the others are deemed good. Suppose Taurus is the rising sign. Then Jupiter a natural benefic would not be deemed good in Scorpio in the seventh house (governing matrimonial affairs) because Jupiter would be the lord of the eight in seventh. Suppose the rising sign is Virgo and Mars in seventh in Pisces. Mars would be very evil because he is a natural malefic besides being lord of the third (Scorpio) and eighth (Aries). These shades of qualities must not be overlooked.

(*ii*) The house should have the aspect of benefics and not of malefics. Here also natural benefics which are lords of good houses come in the first category and natural benefics if they happen to be lords of evil houses in the particular chart come in the second category. The aspect of natural malefics are evil but not so evil if they happen to be lords of good houses in the chart under examination. But if the natural malefics also became the lords of evil houses in the chart, they become very evil. There is one exception to the above rule. If the lord of a house whether a benefic or a malefic aspects his own house it is always deemed good. So also the aspect of the lord of the ascendant.

(*iii*) The house should not be hemmed in between malefics. This damages the house. On the contrary, if hemmed in between benefics, it increases the efficacy. Suppose we are judging the fourth house for a Leo ascendant. Then Scorpio would fall in the fourth house. Now if Jupiter is say in 13°, Libra and Mercury in 20th degree Sagittarius, then the fourth house Scorpio would be hemmed in between benefics. But if in the above illustration, suppose Rahu occupies 28th degree in Libra then Scorpio would not be deemed hemmed in between benefics, because the immediately preceding planet in Libra is Rahu and not Jupiter. This factor must also be taken into account as in the context of planet being hemmed in between benefics and malefics discussed earlier.

(*iv*) Mantreshwar in his *Phala Deepika* Chapter XV Verses 2, 6 and 7 states that benefics in 2nd, 4th, 5th, 7th, 9th and 10th as counted from the house under consideration enhance the well-being of the house under consideration. Malefics in 4th, 5th, 8th, 9th and 12th from a house damage it. Malefics in the 3rd, 6th and 11th from any house are good for it.

Jatakadesh Marga, an old standard work in Sanskrit on predictive astrology states that if malefics are in (*a*) 2nd and 12th, (*b*) 4th and 8th, and (*c*) 5th and 9th, they destroy the good effects of the house. The benefics in the above position enhance the prosperity of the house.

Houses Counted from the Moonsign

The moonsign means the sign in which the Moon was at the time of birth. It is given the same importance in Hindu astrology as the rising sign or the ascendant. Rudra in his Sanskrit commentary on *Horashastra* states on page 23 "50%" effects should be described on the basis of the ascendant and the other

50% on the basis of the moonsign at birth." In our own
experience, we have found that if we arrive at a judgment only
on the basis of the rising sign and the house counted from the
rising sign and the placement of planet therein, the inferences
drawn at times do not agree with the events taking place in the
life of the native. And when we treat the moonsign (called
janma-rashi in Sanskrit) and count the various houses from
there also, the judgment yields far better results. So whatever
guidelines we have provided for judging the lord of houses and
the houses themselves from the ascendant should be applied to
the houses and lords of houses as counted from the moonsign
also and the two sets of inferences—one on the basis of the
ascendant and the other on that of the moonsign should be
synthesised to arrive at the final conclusion.

Karaka

The scrutiny of *Karaka* (significator for a particular matter) is as
important as that of the house and the house lord. We have on
pages 75-77 earlier specified some matters for which one or
more planets are *Karakas*. Broadly speaking, as stated by
Mantreshwer in his *Phala Deepika* Chapter XV verse 17, the
Karakas for the twelve houses are as follows: (1) the Sun (2)
Jupiter (3) Mars (4) the Moon and Mercury (5) Jupiter (6) Mars
and Saturn (7) Venus (8) Saturn (9) the Sun and Jupiter (10) the
Sun, Mercury, Jupiter and Saturn; (11) Jupiter (12) Saturn.

So, When you have to arrive at a judgment examine not only
the first house, and its lord but the Sun also. When you are
considering the second house look not only to the second
house and its lord but to Jupiter also. In regard to *Karaka,* we
have to apply the same tests (*i*) to (*vii*) which we have prescribed
for judging the lord of a house (see pages 83 to 88). We are not
reiterating them. And also the lord of the house should not be
in the 6th, 8th or 12th from the *Karaka* for the house. Generally
the *Karaka* tenanting the house for which he is a *Karaka* is not
favourable. Thus Jupiter in the fifth or Venus in seventh unless
the planet is in its own sign is not desirable. The exceptions are
Mars and Saturn in the sixth; Saturn in eighth; Jupiter in ninth
and Sun, Mercury, Jupiter and Saturn in the tenth.

Body

The first house, its lord and the planets tenanting and aspecting it must be considered. The stature, complexion and the constitution depend in a large measure upon heredity. The Moon, Jupiter and Venus in the first house endow the native with fair complexion. Mars in the first may give wheatish complexion while Saturn, Rahu and Ketu give darkish tinge. Mercury in the first makes one nimble and active. The body takes after the lord of the first house or the lord of the *navansha* falling on the ascending degree.

Parts of the Body

The twelve houses—first to twelfth have correlation with different parts of the body as follows:

House	Part	House	Part
I	head	VII	basti
II	face[1]	VIII	genitals
III	chest[2]	IX	thighs
IV	heart	X	knees
V	stomach	XI	calves
VI	navel	XII	feet

The houses second to sixth represent the limbs on the right side while houses eighth to twelfth govern the left. The latter half of the first house and the first half of the seventh represent the right side while the first half of the first and the later half of the seventh govern the left.

Western astrologers relate throat and neck to the second house, but Hindu astrologers assign it to the third. *Basti* is a Sanskrit word. For its meaning readers are referred to page 29.

Aries, Taurus, Aquarius and Pisces are short signs; Gemini, Cancer, Sagittarius and Capricorn are medium-sized; while Leo, Virgo, Libra and Scorpio long. If a short sign falls on a house and the lord of the house tenants a short sign that part of the

---

1. Also eyes, mouth, tongue.
2. Also ears, Shoulders and arms.

body will be small. Suppose Aries is the ascendant and Mars lord of Aries tenants Pisces then Aries and Pisces both being short signs, the head (because the first house governs the head) will be small.

Temperament

For temperament, we must examine the effects of the various planets in signs and houses, but it primarily depends upon the first house, its lord and the planets tenanting and aspecting the first house. The Sun gives imperiousness, the Moon flexibility, Mars imparts anger, Mercury makes one mirthful, Jupiter endows wisdom and sagacity, Venus makes amiable and pleasure-seeking, while Saturn inclines one to be reserved, sober and suspicious. These effects must be blended with the effects due to Moon—his sign and house position and his conjunction with or the aspects he receives from other planets.

Diseases

Any house tenanted or aspected by a natural malefic will cause ailment in that part of the body. Look to the chapter on houses and mark which part of the body each house indicates. Thus the second and the twelfth houses, tenanted by malefics, or malefics, in the eighth and sixth and respectively fully aspecting the second and the twelfth damage the eyesight. Sun and Venus or Moon and Venus together in the sixth or the twelfth damage the left eye while these in the eighth or second impair the vision in the right eye. Venus in these houses has propensity to impair the vision. The twelfth house also governs teeth. Malefics tenanting the fifth or malefics in the eleventh fully aspecting the fifth, give stomach trouble. Malefics in the eighth particularly Mars there causes piles or fistula in the anus and diseases due to the corruption of blood. Affliction to the Moon and the fourth house may cause heart trouble. The Sun in Aquarius in the first house also causes heart trouble. Affliction of Mercury may give nervous trouble or even mental trouble such as schizophrenia. Affliction to Moon and Mercury both causes insanity; Mars causes boils, wounds, fevers, cuts; Venus gives diseases of the urinary tract—prostrate gland, kidney spematorrhoea. Jupiter causes diseases due to good living such as blood pressure. Saturn causes ailments due to want of nutrition or faulty assimilation. In the Hindu system of medicine called *ayurveda* diseases are caused by the imbalance of one or more of the three humours, (*i*) *vata* (wind), (*ii*)*pitta* (bile) and (*iii*) *kapha* (phlegm). The allocation of the humours to the various planets is as follows: Sun—bile; Moon—wind and phlegm; Mars—bile; Mercury—wind, bile and phlegm; Jupiter—phlegm; Venus—wind and phlegm; Saturn—wind. Rahu is like Saturn. Ketu is like Mars. If any planet is lord of the second, third, sixth, eighth, eleventh and twelfth—weak by sign, in an unfavourable house and aspected by a malefic and in particular if the aspecting planet be lord of an evil house, the native may suffer from disease arising out of the imbalance of wind, bile or phlegm according to afflicted planet.

In examining, the chart for diseases, the readers are advised to scrutinise Mars and Saturn and the sixth house and the lord thereof. Even the lord of the first occupying the 6th, 8th or 12th house and in conjunction with a malefic impairs health. Also there is an analogy between the signs and parts of body as given earlier on page 29. To clarify, if the sign Aries tenants malefics and is aspected by malefics, there may be diseases or hurt in the head including brain trouble.

Wealth

Look to houses second, fourth, fifth, ninth and eleventh and Jupiter significator of wealth. There is a Sanskrit word *sambandha,* which in the astrological context means as follows: Two planets A and B are deemed to have *sambandha* if (*i*) A and B occupy the same sign, (*ii*) A and B have full mutual aspect on each other, (*iii*) A is in the sign owned by B and B occupies the sign owned by A, or (*iv*) (*a*) A occupies the sign owned by B and fully aspects B, or (*b*) A fully aspects B, who occupies the sign owned by A.

This technical word must be kept in memory, for we shall have occasion to refer to it in subsequent pages.

Lords of houses, whose *sambandha* as explained above is conducive to wealth are as follows:

(*i*) 1 and 2, (*ii*) 1 and 4, (*iii*) 1 and 5, (*iv*) 1 and 9, (*v*) 1 and 10, (*vi*) 1 and 11, (*vii*) 2 and 4, (*viii*) 2 and 5, (*ix*) 2 and 9, (*x*) 2 and 10 (*xi*) 2 and 11, (*xii*) 4 and 5, (*xiii*) 4 and 9, (*xiv*) 4 and 10, (*xv*) 4 and 11, (*xvi*) 5 and 9, (*xvii*) 5 and 10, (*xviii*) 5 and 11, (*xix*) 9 and 10, and (*xx*) 9 and 11 (xxi) 10 and 11.

Stronger these planets are by house, sign and more benefic aspects they receive, better it is for wealth.

Poverty

The conjunction, exchange of place or mutual full aspect between the lords of the following houses inclines to poverty or want of wealth:

(*i*) 1 and 6, (*ii*) 2 and 6, (*iii*) 3and 6, (*iv*) 4 and 6, (*v*) 5 and6, (*vi*) 7 and 6, (*vii*) 8 and 6, (*viii*) 9 and 6, (*ix*) 10 and 6, (*x*) 11 and 6, (*xi*) 12 and 6, (*xii*) 8 and 12, (*xiii*) 1 and 12, (*xiv*) 2 and 12, (*xv*) 3 and 12, (*xvi*) 4 and 12, (*xvii*) 5 and 12, (*xviii*) 7 and 12, (*xix*) 9 and12, (*xx*) 10 and 12, and (*xxi*)11and 12.

It is difficult to find a chart in which there may be exclusively good combinations or bad ones. So the readers have to balance them and arrive at the resultant conclusion. Besides, it also happens that a person may have wealth and affluence during the periods of palnets which cause richness and may suffer from poverty during the periods of adverse planets. For influence of periods, readers are referred to Chapter X.

If the Moon, Jupiter and Venus are weak and afflicted they also lead to want of wealth. The eleventh house stands for income, the second for accumulated wealth, the ninth for general prosperity and the fourth for immovable properties. Benefics in the 1st and 2nd bring money. Planets whether benefics or malefics in the eleventh bring income. Benefics in the twelfth are not evil, but malefics there destroy wealth. Malefics in the second—particularly if lords of sixth, eighth or twelfth also lead to dissipation of wealth.

Immovable Properties

Immovable property is judged from the fourth house, its lord and Mars. If the fourth house, its lord and Mars. If the fourth house is weak and the eighth house strong, the native sells away his ancestral house and builds a new one. If the lord of the first is conjoined with the lord of the fourth—particularly in the fourth house—there is sudden acquisition of immovable property.

Speech
Speech and eloquence are judged from the second house and Mercury. Both strong, and well aspected endow the native with eloquence. But it must be noted that malefics tenanting or aspecting the second would give harsh speech, while if benefics tenant or aspect the house, the speech would be sweet and amiable.

Brothers and Sisters
These are judged from the third house and Mars, who is a *karaka* for them. If the third house and its lord are strong and Mars is afflicted or *vice versa* there may be only partial happiness, if both are afflicted, there is practically no happiness in this regard. Malefics in the third increase one's own valour but are evil for the longevity of co-borns or one does not have cordial relations with them. Male planets tenanting or aspecting the third house give more brothers. Female or eunuch planets give more sisters.

Mother
The mother is judged from the Moon and the fourth house. A severe affliction to both indicates premature death of mother. If malefics tenant the fourth house one may not have cordial relations with one's mother. So is the position when the Moon is ill-placed and aspected by malefics. The relationship between the lords of the first and fourth should also be examined.

Conveyances
Conveyances are judged from the fourth house and Venus. In determining whether one will have cars, the general appraisal of wealth and station in life also constitute a factor. For some

people, purchase of a couple of cars annually is a matter of routine for others it is beyond their expectations. So the state of wealth has also to be considered.

Friends
Western astrologers judge friends from the eleventh house, but in Hindu astrology an estimate of friends is made from the fourth and Mercury. Venus must also be considered because Venus in a native determines his capacity to co-operate with others—particularly with women. If the lord of the first house is strong and well-placed having *sambandha* with strong benefics the native associates with well-placed and high people, but if the lord of the first is weak and ill-aspected and has *sambandha* with weak malefics, he associates with low people; nor are his friends reliable.

Happiness
Home and happiness—both are judged from the fourth house. If the lords of the first and the fourth are strong and have *sambandha* with benefics, the native is happy. Malefics tenanting the first house or aspecting the lord of the first house and the Moon make one disgruntled and unhappy. With Venus strong, one enjoys life and that is a contributory factor to happiness. With an afflicted Venus, one lacks enjoyment though he may have money and means in plenty. Further, a person may be happy when he is having good periods and unhappy during the tenure of evil ones. For periods, please refer to Chapter X.

Education
Education is judged from the fifth house and its lord. Jupiter is a *karaka* for wisdom and Mercury for intelligence. These two planets must be given due consideration along with the planets tenanting the fifth house and aspecting it. Of course, the lord of the fifth house has to be judged in all his bearings. The southern Indian school judges education from fourth.

Children

Children are judged from the fifth house, its lord and Jupiter. Malefics tenanting or aspecting the fifth house destroy children or cause sickness to them. If the lords of the first and the fifth are friends and mutually aspect each other or are conjoined or are great friends, there is generally cordiality between the native and his children. If they are great enemies and in sixth and eighth from each other, one's children are refractory to the native.

Gain from Betting

Gain from betting, speculation, races, lotteries—sudden expected gains, other than by inheritance, are judged from the fifth house and its lord. But the first consideration should be whether the chart indicates wealth. If the fifth house is strong, tenanted and aspected by benefics and the lord of the fifth also strong, tenanting the seconds or the eleventh house and receiving the aspect of benefics, the native may have sudden gains. But when reverse is the case that is, the fifth house is afflicted and the lord of the fifth in twelfth and conjoined with or aspected by malefics, the native loses in speculation. The Moon or Rahu in the fifth gives a great desire for speculation.

Enemies

For considering this astrological factor, we have to take into account the sixth house, its lord, Mars and Saturn. If these are strong, one generally triumphs over his enemies, but along with these, the first house and its lord must also be strong. If the first house and its lord are weak and the lord of the sixth stronger than the lord of the first, one is always troubled by his enemies. A strong Mars annihilates enemies. So does a strong Saturn.

Wife

The wife is to be judged from the seventh house, its lord and Venus. When Venus is strong one has much enjoyment. The seventh house also stands for sexual pleasures. When the seventh house, its lord and Venus are weak, one does not have much sex enjoyment. For pleasures of the bed (sex) we look to the twelfth house also. Venus, if placed in twelfth is a guarantee for pleasures of the bed (including extra-marital). If the lord of the seventh is stronger than the lord of the first, one marries in a family higher than one's own. Malefics in the first, second, fourth, seventh, eighth and twelfth make one lose one's wife prematurely unless this evil in one's chart is set off by malefics tenanting the above houses in the wife's chart. For judging the husband, apply the same rules as have been prescribed for judging the wife. And in addition her Jupiter should also be examined. Jupiter is *karaka* for husband.

Longevity

Detailed calculations and elaborate rules have been laid down in ancient texts to determine longevity, but these cannot be reproduced in this book. So the readers will do well to give attention to the following factors which ensure good longevity:

(*i*)   The first house and its lord should be strong and both of these should be aspected by benefics.

(*ii*) The benefics should be strong and perferably in angles or trines.

(*iii*) The malefics should be in the third, sixth and eleventh houses.

(*iv*) The lord of the eighth should be fairly strong but not stronger than the lord of the first. The lord of the eighth should also be conjoined with or aspected by benefics.

(*v*)   The eighth house should receive the aspect of the benefics.

(*vi*) The Moon should be strong and conjoined with and/or aspected by benefics. When the Moon is weak and afflicted, generally the native dies during childhood.

(*vii*) The lord of the eighth in the third from the ascendant or Saturn in the eighth also confers good longevity.

Determination of exact time of death has eluded even expert and experienced astrologers but if the above rules are kept in mind, the readers would be able to determine fairly well, whether the longevity is long, medium or short. To determine the time of death according to the period and sub-period of planets has been discussed in Chapter X.

Legacy

For judging legacy or gain by inheritance the first consideration should be whether the native has a rich relation from whom he can expect a legacy. Legacies do not drop from heaven. All persons, do inherit from their parents, husband, wife and other close relations whose successors they are, but if the gain is only normal, there would be nothing in the chart to indicate it. For legacies, worth the name, the eighth house and its lord should be strong. The lord of the eighth in second or eleventh or the lord of the second or eleventh strong and posited in the eighth and the aspects of the benefics on the eighth and its lord bring legacy.

Religiousness

Some people are more religious than others. Some are positively irreligious. Much depends upon the country and times also. In the communist countries most of the people do not believe in God. In India by heredity and tradition people are religious. But the younger generation is sniffing at older values. All these should be kept in mind. The ninth house stands for religion and the fifth for devotion. Jupiter is the *karaka* for religion. If these are strong, a person is religious. The tenancy of Saturn and Rahu in the ninth makes one religiously wayward. Saturn's aspect does the same. Saturn inclines one to be more philosophical than religious. Jupiter in the ascendant, third, fifth or ninth or Jupiter conjoined with the Moon or his aspect on the ninth house from the Moon makes one religious.

Foreign Travel

Foreign Travel is judged from the ninth and the twelfth. Benefics in the ninth bring gain from foreigners or foreign lands. If the lord of the ninth is in twelfth or the lord of the twelfth in ninth, the native goes abroad. Planets in the eighth, if benefic and strong bring gain from across the waters.

Father

Father is judged from the tenth house and the Sun. If the lord of the tenth and the tenth house are strong and so is the Sun, there is good longevity for father. When malefics tenant or aspect the tenth house or afflict the lord of the tenth or the Sun, father's longevity is curtailed or he does not pull on well with his father. For determining whether the native would have cordial relationship with father, relationship between the lords of the first and tenth should be examined. The Sun is debilitated in Libra and generally natives born with Sun in Libra do not pull on well with their fathers. In south India, the astrologers judge the father from the ninth house instead of the tenth.

Career

Career can be classified into four main groups: (*i*) agriculture, (*ii*) service, (*iii*) independent profession, and (*iv*) trade and commerce. Formerly in India, the career depended mostly on heredity. Now more and more people are taking up new lines. Still, heredity, qualifications, aptitude and general background should be kept in mind.

For agriculture, the fourth house or the lord thereof should have some connection with the second, ninth or eleventh houses or the lords there of. Venus is connected with wet lands; Saturn is associated with agriculture. Mars has been in Hindu mythology called the son of the earth. So these should also be considered.

For service the third, sixth and the tenth houses and lords thereof should be judged. The lord of the first in the third or the sixth inclines to service. Planets in the third also do the same. The lord of the third or sixth in the tenth or eleventh may also indicate gain from service.

We have observed that Scorpio ascendant or the Moon in Scorpio also inclines to a career of service. Mars in the first, third or tenth or Mars strong anywhere in the chart makes one enter the military or police service where one has to bear arms. Alternately one may follow a line connected with fire (factories).

For trade and commerce or independent profession such as that of a doctor or an advocate, no set rules can be provided.

Persons whose lord of the seventh house is weak or the seventh house afflicted, due to tenancy of malefics should not enter into partnership business.

Generally when the ninth and the tenth houses and their lords are strong, the native occupies a good position in his career. For political career the Sun should also be strong. To become a peoples' representative *i.e.*, a career depending upon success in an election by people, the Moon should be strong. The Sun represents the classes—Moon the masses.

Good Yogas

General guidelines for the appraisal of the birth chart and the various departments of life have been discussed. We will now discuss *yogas*. *Yoga* is a Sanskrit word meaning addition of two or more factors. There is another word *rajayoga* which means combining of two or more factors which lifts the native to a high position in life. These are:

1. *Sambandha* between the lords of the following houses: (*i*) 1 and 5, (*ii*) 1 and 9, (*iii*)1 and 4, (*iv*)1 and 7, (*v*) 1 and 10, (*vi*) 4 and 5, (*vii*) 4 and 9, (*viii*) 5 and 7, (*ix*) 5 and 10, (*x*) 7 and 9, (*xi*) 9 and 10, are very good *rajayogas* provided the combination does not have *sambandha* with the lords of 3, 6, 8, and 11. For *sambandha* see page 91. For Aries ascendant, conjunction of Mars and Saturn (lords of the first and tenth houses respectively) in the fifth would be a good *rajayoga* but two malefics Mars and Saturn in the fifth would damage the prospects of children, because from the fifth we judge children, So a *yoga* may be good for certain purposes; for others it may not be so. These subtle shades should be kept in mind.

2. Benefic or benefics in the twelfth from the moonsign or benefic or benefics in the second from the moonsign or on both sides (adjoining signs) of the Moon.

3. Benefic or benefics other than Moon in the twelfth from the sunsign or benefic or benefics other than the Moon in the second from sunsign or on both sides *i.e.*, the second

and the twelfth. The presence of the Moon in the second or the twelfth does not constitute the *yoga,* but it does not mar it either.

In 1 and 2 above Mars or Saturn on either side of the moonsign or sunsign or on both sides, constitute the yoga but it is better to have benefics than malefics as constituents of the *yoga.*

4. Benefics in the 3rd, 6th, 10th or 11th from the ascendant.
5. Benefics in the 3rd, 6th, 10th or 11th from the moonsign.

In 4 and 5 above maximum good effects will be felt if all the benefics occupy any of the above houses, together or separately; if only two do so, the result will still be good; with only one benefic in the above position, the benefit will be in lesser measure.

6. If the Moon is in his own *navansha* or his great friend's *navansha,* and he is aspected
   (*i*) by jupiter if the birth be during day.
   (*ii*) by Venus, if the birth be at night.
   (Sunrise to sunset is treated as day; sunset to sunrise as night.)
7. If Mercury, Jupiter and Venus occupy the 6th, 7th, 8th from the ascendant.
8. If Mercury, Jupiter and Venus occupy the 6th, 7th and 8th from moonsign.

In 7 and 8 above Mercury, Jupiter and Venus need not be in the 6th, 7th or 8th in any particular order. Two or even three planets may be in any of the above houses.

9. In case of birth-charts of males,
   (*i*) the birth should be during day.
   (*ii*) the ascendant, the Sun and the Moon—all the three should be in odd signs.
10. In the case of birth charts of females,
   (*i*) the birth should be at night
   (*ii*) the ascendant, the Sun and the Moon—all the three should be in female (even) signs.

11. Mercury, Jupiter and Venus all the three should be in angles (*i.e.,* in the 1st, 4th, 7th or 10th from the ascendant). One or more planet may be together. The *yoga* becomes still better if Mars is in the tenth.

12. Mars in Aries, Scorpio or Capricorn in 1st, 4th, 7th or 10th, from the ascendant or the Moon.

13. Mercury in Gemini or Virgo in 1st, 4th, 7th or 10th from the ascendant or the Moon.

14. Jupiter in Cancer, Sagittarius or Pisces in 1st, 4th, 7th, or 10th from the ascendant or the Moon.

15. Venus in Taurus, Libra or Pisces in 1st, 4th, 7th or 10th from the ascendant or the Moon.

16. Saturn in Libra, Capricorn or Aquarius in 1st, 4th, 7th or 10th from the ascendant or the Moon.

17. The Moon and Mars together in a sign.

18. Jupiter in 1st, 4th, 7th or 10th from the moonsign.

The Moon and Jupiter in Cancer in the first or the fourth house would be a powerful *yoga,* because the Moon would be in his own sign and Jupiter exalted therein. Also, it will be a conjunction of the lords of good houses. But suppose the Moon is in Scorpio and Jupiter in Taurus. The two will still be in mutual angles but Jupiter will be in his natural enemy's sign and the Moon debilitated. Thus these shades of difference should not be overlooked.

19. Rahu or Ketu in an angle (1st, 4th, 7th or 10th from the ascendant) conjoined with the lord of the 5th or 9th.

20. Rahu or Ketu in a trine (5th or 9th from the ascendant) conjoined with the lord of an angle.

21. If Jupiter be the lord of 2nd or 5th or 11th and if the lord of the 2nd or 9th or 11th is an angle from the moonsign.

22. If the Sun be in *vargottama* except in Libra and the Moon in Cancer.

23. If the Moon and Jupiter are in their own signs and occupy an angle or a trine (one in an angle and other in a trine).

24. If the full Moon is an angle and is aspected both by Jupiter and Venus.

25. Full Moon in Taurus.

All the above twenty-five *yogas* lead to wealth, prosperity and good position in life. But in assessing the strength of the above *yogas*, the same tests hould be applied as have been prescribed earlier for judging the lords of houses.

There is one more overriding consideration for judging the *yogas*, in which the Moon is a constituent. The Moon is considered weak if either of the following factors is present and the *yoga* effects are considerably impaired.

(*i*)   If the Moon has less than five digits. This condition obtains from the 10th day of the dark fortnight to the fifth day of the bright fortnight.

(*ii*) When the birth is during day (from sunrise to sunset)and the Moon is above the horizon. How to know that the Moon is above the horizon ? The part of the zodiac commencing from the ascending degree to 180° *i.e.* to the descending degree *i.e.* the degree of the ecliptic on the western horizon—constitutes half of the zodiac. In the example horoscope (page 16) the 27th degree of Cancer is rising. So 27° to 30°. Cancer, Leo, Virgo, Libra, Scorpio, Sagittarius and the first 27° of Capricorn constitute half of the zodiac, below the earth. The rest 27° to 30° Capricorn, Aquarius, Pisces, Aries, Taurus, Gemini and 0° to 27° Cancer are above the horizon. If both the factors are present the good effects prescribed for the *yoga* are practically eroded.

CHAPTER IX

PLANETARY PERIODS

In western astrology, predictions are made on the basis of directions and transits. Even in directions four sets are used—the primary directions—progressed and converse and secondary directions progressed and converse. But in Hindu astrology the predictions are based on periods and sub-periods—called *mahadashas* and *antardashas* respectively, and of course transits are utilised as an aid to supplement the inferences drawn from the *mahadashas* and *antardashas*. The *mahadasha* is generally referred to as *dasha* and the *antardasha* as *antar*. In south India the *antardasha* is referred to as *bhukti*. We are however, using here the word period for *mahadasha* and sub-period for the *antardasha*.

There are several kinds of periods and sub-periods prescribed in standard works on the subject. *Parashar* who flourished several thousand years ago and is in a way deemed father of Hindu astrology has laid down rules for calculating and interpreting forty-two kinds of periods but with the passage of time, many of these have been abandoned by practising Hindu astrologers. Only a few survived. The *ashtottari*—meaning totalling to 108 years—is still followed in Bengal and western India—particularly in Gujarat.

But even for calculating *ashtottari* there are two methods. The one followed in Bengal is different from that followed in Gujarat. The *tribhagi* period is followed in Nepal and the *yogini* in Kashmir and Himachal.

But the most popular and the most prevalent system of periods followed in India is the *Vinshottari* which means constituting one hundred and twenty years. Since it is almost universally followed in India, we are now dealing with it.

The periods for which the various planets hold sway and the order in which they follow is as follows:

Table A

	Planet	Period		Planet	Period
1.	Sun	6 years	6.	Saturn	19 years
2.	Moon	10 years	7.	Mercury	17 years
3.	Mars	7 years	8.	Ketu	7 years
4.	Rahu	18 years	9.	Venus	20 years
5.	Jupiter	16 years			
				Total	120 years

Readers will have noticed that the above order of planets is not in conformity with the sequence of planets presiding over the week days (and possibly could not be because Rahu and Ketu have no week days allotted to them), nor are they in any other known order. We also notice that there appears to be no apparent logic in the lengths of the periods allotted to the various planets. Why should the sun—round which the other planets revolve, get a period of only 6 years, while Venus should get the longest one—that is of 20 years?

Many authors have put forward their reasoning—in all cases far-fetched—to explain the above order and duration periods, but the whole problem remains an occult mystery.

Each of these periods given in Table A above is further sub-divided into 9 sub-periods. The period of Sun—constituting 6 years has 9 sub-periods—the first one being his own and then of Moon, Mars, Rahu *etc.* in the order given above. The Moon's period—constituting 10 years—is also sub-divided into 9 periods—the first sub-period being his own, and then of Mars, Rahu, Jupiter, Saturn, Mercury *etc.* And so with other periods. Thus, each planet's period is divided into 9 sub-periods—the first sub-period being its own—and then of the other planets in the order given in Table A above.

Astrologers further sub-divided each sub-period into 9 sub-periods and these are called *pratyantardashas* or *pratyantar,* but we do not propose to go into such minute details in this book. We shall confine ourselves in this book to periods and sub-periods only.

And what is the duration of the sub-period of a planet in each period? It is worked out on the basis of rule of three. Let us clarify it by taking a specific example.

What would be Rahu's sub-period in the period of Venus?

When the total is 120 years Rahu gets 18 years.

When the total is 1 year Rahu gets 18/120 years.

Therefore, when the total is 20 years Rahu gets 18/120x20/1= 3 years.

So Rahu's sub-period will be of 3 years in the period of Venus.

The table given below of Sub-periods in the period of planets is to serve as a readyreckoner and save time in calculation:

Table B

1. *Sun*		2. *Moon*	
	Y.M.D.		*Y.M.D.*
Sun	0- 3-18	Moon	0-10-0
Moon	0- 6- 0	Mars	0- 7-0
Mars	0- 4- 6	Rahu	1- 6-0
Rahu	0-10-24	Jupiter	1- 4-0
Jupiter	0- 9-18	Saturn	1- 7-0
Saturn	0-11-12	Mercury	1- 5-0
Mercury	0-10- 6	Ketu	0- 7-0
Ketu	0- 4- 6	Venus	1- 8-0
Venus	1- 0- 0	Sun	0- 6-0
Total	6 years	Total	10 years

3. *Mars*		4. *Rahu*	
	Y.M.D.		*Y.M.D.*
Mars	0- 4-27	Rahu	2- 8-12
Rahu	1- 0-18	Jupiter	2- 4-24
Jupiter	0-11- 6	Saturn	2-10- 6
Saturn	1- 1- 9	Mercury	2- 6-18
Mercury	0-11-27	Ketu	1- 0-18
Ketu	0- 4-27	Venus	3- 0- 0
Venus	1- 2- 0	Sun	0-10-24
Sun	0- 4- 6	Moon	1- 6- 0
Moon	0- 7- 0	Mars	1- 0-18
Total	7 years	Total	18 years

5. *Jupiter*			6. *Saturn*	
	Y.M.D.			*Y.M.D.*
Jupiter	2- 1-18		Saturn	3- 0- 3
Saturn	2- 6-12		Mercury	2- 8- 9
Mercury	2- 3- 6		Ketu	1-1- 9
Ketu	0-11- 6		Venus	3- 2- 0
Venus	2- 8- 0		Sun	0-11-12
Sun	0- 9-18		Moon	1- 7- 0
Moon	1- 4- 0		Mars	1- 1- 9
Mars	0-11- 6		Rahu	2-10- 6
Rahu	2- 4-24		Jupiter	2- 6-12
Total	16 years		Total	19 years

7. *Mercury*			8. *Ketu*	
	Y.M.D.			*Y.M.D.*
Mercury	2- 4-27		Ketu	0- 4-27
Ketu	0-11-27		Venus	1- 2- 0
Venus	2-10- 0		Sun	0- 4- 6
Sun	0-10- 6		Moon	0- 7- 0
Moon	1- 5- 0		Mars	0- 4-27
Mars	0-11-27		Rahu	1- 0- 18
Rahu	2- 6-18		Jupiter	0-11- 6
Jupiter	2- 3- 6		Saturn	1- 1- 9
Saturn	2- 8- 9		Mercury	0-11-27
Total	17 years		Total	7 years

9. *Venus*	
	Y.M.D.
Venus	3-4-0
Sun	1- 0-0
Moon	1-8- 0
Mars	1-2-0-
Rahu	3-0-0
Jupiter	2-8-0
Saturn	3- 2-0
Mercury	2-10-0
Ketu	1- 2-0
Total	20 years

* *Y.M.D.* means years, months and days respectively.

What is the idea in having periods of planets and then 9 sub-periods in each of the planet's period ? The question is a very relevant one and we shall discuss the whole matter in a subsequent chapter. In this chapter we are giving instructions in regard to only calculations of periods and sub-periods.

The Period at Birth

We have given in Table A, the planetary periods of planets. In Table B we have specified the durations of sub-periods. The next step to explain is : which was the period at birth ? In order to understand that we have to bear in mind that the period at birth is determined by the longitude of the Moon in the radix.[1]

The zodiac constitutes 360 degrees. These 360 degrees are divided into 27 equal sectors—each constituting 13°-20'. Each sector is presided by a *nakshatra*. The word *nakshatra* in *Sanskrit* means a constellation or an asterism. Below are being given the longitudes in the zodiac and the names of the *nakshatras* which preside over the 27 equal sectors. Against each *nakshatra* has been specified the name of the planet, whose period will be current at birth if the longitude of the Moon was in the domain of the particular *nakshatra*.

Table C

Longitudes, Nakshatras and the Planets

Longitude		Nakshatra	Planet
S.D.M.	S.D.M.[2]		
0- 0- 0 to	0-13-20	Ashwini	Ketu
0-13-20 to	0-26-40	Bharani	Venus
0-26-40 to	1-10- 0	Krittika	Sun
1-10- 0 to	1-23-20	Rohini	Moon
1-23-20 to	2- 6-40	Mrigashira	Mars
2- 6-40 to	2-20- 0	Ardra	Rahu
2-20- 0 to	3- 3-20	Punarvasu	Jupiter

1. Radix in astrology means the horoscope of birth or birth-chart-longitudes of planets and cusps of the houses at birth; radical means pertaining to the radix.
2. *S.D.M.* Means sign, degrees and minutes.

3- 3-20 to	3-16-40	Pushya	Saturn
3-16-40 to	4- 0- 0	Ashlesha	Mercury
4- 0- 0 to	4-13-20	Magha	Ketu
4-13-20 to	4-26-40	Poorva Phalguni	Venus
4-26-40 to	5-10-0	Uttara Phalguni	Sun
5-10- 0 to	5-23-20	Hasta	Moon
5-23-20 to	6- 6-40	Chitra	Mars
6- 6-40 to	6-20- 0	Swati	Rahu
6-20- 0 to	7- 3-20	Vishakha	Jupiter
7- 3-20 to	7-16-40	Anuradha	Saturn
7- 16-40 to	8- 0- 0	Jyeshtha	Mercury
8- 0- 0 to	8-13-20	Moola	Ketu
8-13-20 to	8-26-40	Poorvashadha	Venus
8-26-40 to	9-10- 0	Uttarashadha	Sun
9-10- 0 to	9-23-20	Shravana	Moon
9-23-20 to	10- 6-40	Dhanishtha	Mars
10- 6-40 to	10-20- 0	Shatabhisha	Rahu
10-20- 0 to	11- 3-20	Poorva bhadra	Jupiter
11- 3-20 to	11-16-40	Uttara bhadra	Saturn
11-16-40 to	12- 0- 0	Revati	Mercury

The Sanskrit names of the *nakshatras* have been furnished but it is really not necessary to commit them to memory. What is actually required to keep in mind is that if the longitude of the Moon at birth is say between 4-26°-40' and 5-10°-0' (*i.e.* between 26°-40' of Leo and 10° Virgo) the native will at birth have the Sun's period. Or take another example; if say at birth the longitude of the Moon was 11-16°-40' to 12°-0°-0' (*i.e.* between 16°-40' and 30° of Pisces) the native at birth had Mercury's period.

Another point to remember is that if the native is born when the Moon's longitude is say 16°-40' in Pisces *i.e.* Just at the commencement of the sector (refer to the table above) he will have the full quota of Mercury's period or 17 years. But suppose the native was born when the Moon's longitude was 23°-20' in Pisces (*i.e.* the mid-point between 16°-40' and 30° of Pisces), he will have only half the quota or Mercury's period left. So, he will have $8^{1/2}$ years of mercury's period at birth, then 7 years of Ketu's period, then 20 years of period of Venus, then 6 years of Sun and so on. Only that person who lives for 120 years can have the full quota or periods of all the nine planets. Others have periods of only 4, 5, 6, 7, or 8 planets.

Example:

In order that readers may become well-acquainted with the process of working out the balance of the planetary period at birth, we are taking up the birth data of the native, whose chart has been worked out in Chapter II earlier.

Please remember that for working out the planetary periods, only the longitude of the Moon in the sidereal zodiac is required and nothing else.

Each *nakshatra* covers 13°-20'. Since each degree constitutes 60 minutes 13°-20' = 13x60+20=800'. If the native is born at the commencement of Ashwini, Magha or Mool full balance of 800' will initially give Ketu's period extending to 7 years; if the native is born at the beginning of Bharani, Poorvaphalguni or Poorvashadha, there will be the period of Venus for 20 years commencing from birth. If the native is born when the Moon has just entered Krittika, Uttaraphalguni or Uttarashadha, the child will have on initial period of the Sun for 6 years and so on. The planet whose period will be current at birth depends upon the Moon's position in a particular *nakshatra*. The name of the *nakshatra* and against it the name of the planet, whose period will be the first one, have been stated in Table C on page 107 and are not being repeated.

Balance of Period at Birth

But the native gets the full quota of the planet's period only if the Moon has just entered it. If at birth the Moon has covered one fourth of the sector (over which a particular *nakshatra* has domain), and he has to travel only three fourths of it, the native will have only three fourths of the full quota of the planet's period. This point must be fully grasped. We shall further clarify it by working out the balance of the first period at birth, in the example horoscope.

Reference to page 21 would show that the Moon's longitude at birth was 8-0°-24'. Further reference to Table C on page 107 would show that longitudes from 8-0°-0' to 8-13°-20', are under the domain of Moola *nakshatra*. Since each *nakshatra* has domain over 800' we have to find how much has the Moon to travel. We proceed as follows:

Degree where Moola ends	8-13°-20'
Degree of Moon at birth	8- 0°-24'
Balance distance	0-12°-56'

Only 12°-56' remain to be covered by the Moon. Now we calculate as follows: we convert 12°-56' into minutes. 12 x 60+56=776'. Now, we work out by rule of there:

For 800 minutes the quota is 7 years

$$\text{"} \quad 1' \quad \text{"} \quad \text{"} \quad \text{"} \quad \text{"} \quad \frac{7}{800} \text{ years}$$

$$\text{"} \quad 776' \quad \text{"} \quad \text{"} \quad \text{"} \quad \text{"} \quad \frac{7}{800} \times 776 \text{ years.}$$

$$= 6 \text{ years } 9 \text{ months } 14 \text{ days.}$$

We leave the fraction of the day if it is less than half and treat it as a full day, if it is more than half.

Some readers may raise a doubt: why have we taken above the full quota as 7 years ? because, the Moon was in Moola *nakshatra* at birth and Table C would show that, when a person is born in *Moola*, the period corresponding to it is that of Ketu and Table A would show that the full quota for Ketu's period is 7 years. So in the above example the balance of Ketu's period at birth would be 6 years 9 months 14 days. Now we make the table of periods as follows:

Table of Planetary Periods (Mahadashas)

Planet	Duration Y.M.D.	Till the age of Y.M.D.
Balance of Ketu's period of birth	6-9-14	6-9-14
Period of Venus	20-0- 0	26-9-14
Period of Sun	6-0- 0	32-9-14
Period of Moon	10-0- 0	42-9-14
Period of Mars	7-0- 0	49-9-14
Period of Rahu	18-0- 0	67-9-14
Period of Jupiter	16-0- 0	83-9-14

We have calculated the above period upto the age 83-9-14,

but if the readers want they can add up the period of Saturn (for 19 years, which succeeds Jupiter's period) or still further.

Sub-Periods in the Example Chart

Now we shall explain how to calculate the sub-periods. In the above working of the periods, the readers will have noted that. out of the full quota of 7 years of Ketu the balance at birth was 6 years 9 months 14 days and therefore 2 months 16 days had already elapsed before birth.

Now reference is invited to Table B on page 105-106. If the native had full quota of 7 years of Ketu's period, the initial sub-period would have been Ketu's in his own period, for 4 months 27 days. But 2 months 16 days had already elapsed. So deducting 2 months 16 days out of 4 months 27 days the balance 2 months 11 days only which is the balance of Ketu's sub-period in his own period at birth and we make the table of sub-periods as follows:

Table of Sub-periods (Antardashas) in the Period (Mahadasha) of Ketu

Planet	Duration Y.M.D.	Till the age of Y.M.D.
Balance of Ketu's Sub-period in his own period at birth	0- 2-11	0-2-11
Venus in Ketu	1- 2- 0	1-4-11
Sun "	0- 4- 6	1-8-17
Moon "	0- 7- 0	2-3-17
Mars "	0- 4-27	2-8-14
Rahu "	1- 0-18	3-9- 2
Jupiter "	0-11- 6	4-8- 8
Saturn "	1- 1- 9	5-9-17
Mercury "	0-11-27	6-9-14*

From where have we lifted the sub-periods of Venus, Sun, Moon *etc.* ? From the Table B on page 105-106, having completed the

---

* Attention of beginners is invited that they should check up the sub-period table with the table of major periods and note that the ending age (in the present example 6 years 9 months 14 days) is identical.

table of sub-periods in the first period, the preparation of tables of sub-periods for other periods is easy.

The cycle of planetary periods runs as follows Ketu, Venus, Sun, Moon, Mars, Rahu, Jupiter, Saturn, Mercury, Ketu *etc.*

The first sub-period in a planetary period is its own and then others follows in the cycle stated above. Now we shall work out the table of sub-periods in the period of Venus in the example horoscope. The process is just of simple addition.

Table of Sub-periods (*Antardashas*) in the Period (*Mahadasha*) of Venus

Planet		Duration Y.M.D.	Till the age of Y.M.D.
Venus in Venus		3- 4-0	10- 1-14
Sun	"	1- 0-0	11- 1-14
Moon	"	1- 8-0	12- 9-14
Mars	"	1- 2-0	13-11-14
Rahu	"	3- 0-0	16-11-14
Jupiter	"	2- 8-0	19- 7-14
Saturn	"	3- 2-0	22- 9-14
Mercury	"	2-10-0	25- 7-14
Ketu	"	1- 2-0	26- 9-14

We have added 3 years 4 months to 6 years 9 months 14 days at which age Ketu's period would end and that of Venus would commence to arrive at the age of 10-1-14, when the sub-period of Venus in his own period would end.

In the above manner, tables of sub-period in the subsequent periods of planets can be calculated. The calculation portion has been explained in this chapter; for judgment of periods and sub-periods, the readers are referred to the next chapter.

CHAPTER X

TIMING OF EVENTS

This is one of the most important chapters and much skill and experience are required in applying the rules laid down herein. But the skill and experience presuppose the requirement of tools, because it is only by working with them that efficiency is had. And the tools in the form of rules are being enunciated here. So far, in the preceding chapters we have dealt with 'what'. Now, we are dealing with the correlated question 'when'. It must at the outset be understood that what is not ordained in the birth chart does not come to pass. If a person's chart does not show wealth, even when he is having the periods of most favourable planets, he will not become wealthy, though there may be comparative improvement in his financial affairs. People with their seventh house, the lord thereof and Venus afflicted will not have much matrimonial happiness and even when favourable periods and transits are current, they will not have full conjugal bliss. This basic fact must be always kept in mind.

When judging the events or trend of events during the period or sub-period of planets apply all the rules and interpretations which have been laid down, earlier in regard to location of the planet in sign, house, conjunction or aspects. What the planet is ordained to do in the radix becomes operative when its period or sub-period is current.

In Hindu astrology, timing of events is made on the basis of periods and sub-periods of planets and transits. The calculation of planetary periods and sub-periods has been fully explained in the preceding chapter. To transits, we have devoted an altogether separate chapter—the next one. Here, we confine ourselves to the appraisal of the planetary periods and sub-periods.

How do you appraise a jewel—say a piece of diamond? There are three tests. Along with the size and weight and the lustre we also ensure that it has no blemish—spot or crack *etc.* If we ignore any of the above criteria our judgment may well be off the mark. so, it is in regard to planetary periods. We are laying down three tests—all of which must be applied—if we ignore any one of these, our inference may prove wrong. We shall first discuss the assessment of periods of planets and take up the sub-periods at a subsequent stage. Before we outline the three tests which must be applied to judge a planetary period, the following principles should be kept in mind.

General Principles

1. A planet during its period shows the effects (*i*) of the house or houses it owns, (*ii*) the house it tenants, (*iii*) the house or houses it aspects, (*iv*) the planets it is conjoined with or aspected by.

    Thus, a malefic planet, would during its period damage the house it tenants or the house and houses it aspects. But if the malefic tenants its own house or aspects it, it would not damage it, rather affairs pertaining to that house will prosper. This is on the principle that even a brute does not destroy his own house.

2. When a planet owns two houses it gives during the first half of its period the effects due to ownership of the house which comes first when counted from the ascendant. During the second half of the period, it gives effect due to the ownership of the house which comes later. Thus, if Leo be rising, counting from Leo, Scorpio (falling on the fourth house) comes first and Aries (falling on the ninth house) comes later. So during the first half of his period, Mars will give the result of his lordship of the fourth and during the latter half the effects of his lordship of the ninth. Still to make a finer discrimination his lordship of the *moola trikona* sign is more important than of the other sign. For *moola trikona* sign please refer to pages 41.

3. The effects of planets according as they tenant a sign which rises with front part first or hind part first or both ways has been referred to on pages 34. Reference is invited to these.

4. When a planet owns two signs—one sign falling on a good house and the other of an evil one, if it occupies the sign which falls on a good house—it shows good effect irrespective of its owing the other bad one. Thus, when Virgo is the ascendant Capricorn constitutes the fifth house—a good one and Aquarius, the sixth house—a bad one. But if Saturn lord of Capricorn and Aquarius occupies the fifth house he does not show the evil effect of the ownership of the sixth.

5. In the beginning a planet shows the effect of the house it is in, then of the sign and *navansha* it occupies, and then of the planets conjoined with or aspecting it.

6. If a planet is strong by sign but debilitated in *navansha*, it does not show much good; on the other hand it may show evil results if other factors so warrant.

7. A planet say X if great enemy of planet Y, will during its (X's) period show adverse effect in respect of the house or houses owned by Y. Thus, the period of a planet who is an enemy or a great enemy of the lord of the ascendant is not good.

8. Since Rahu and Ketu do not own any house, Rahu shows the effect of the house he tenants and also of the planet he is conjoined with. So does Ketu.

The First Test

A planet produces effects in regard to matters for which it is a *karaka*. If the planet is strong, good effects will be shown pertaining to matters for which it is a *karaka* but if the planet is weak and afflicted mostly evil effects will follow.

Sun

Thus if the Sun is strong, during his period the native gains money from the king (government), if in government service there may be promotion. The person applies himself to new enterprises daringly and gains money. He becomes famous; his travels are successful. He is victorious in competition, quarrels and litigation. The period proves good for the native's father also.

But if the Sun is weak, there is censure or trouble from government; his travels cause only fatigue and bring no reward; trouble from enemies, fire *etc.* ; he is not courageous; he may suffer in health—there are diseases of the stomach and the heart. Even his father suffers (in health or otherwise).

Moon

When the Moon is strong there is increase in wealth due to peaceful application; increase in family: good food; successful endeavours; favourable for the mother.

When the Moon is weak there is depletion of wealth, mental anguish, troubles in the family; unsavoury food; enmity from one's own people; distress from a powerful opponent; the mother suffers. The native himself may have health trouble due to imbalance of wind and phlegm.

Mars

When Mars is strong, there is gain from government, brothers, land, fire (industries where fire is used), goats and sheep. The native becomes courageous and pushing and successful in his enterprises. There may be gain due to cruel acts or by dubious practices.

But when Mars is weak, there may be quarrels and litigation, in which the native suffers; liaison with a low woman and loss thereby; quarrel with brothers or loss of a brother. The native's dealings become sharp and harsh and he becomes unpopular; enmity with wife, children and senior members; illness to the native due to cuts, wounds, accidents, boils and corruption of blood.

Mercury

When Mercury is strong there is gain from friends or through them, from publications; acting as a middle man or broker or by writing and travelling, domestic happiness; the native's business deals are successful; there is increase in intelligence and learning and he gains name and fame.

When Mercury is weak the native indulges only in crude jokes *i.e.,* his intelligence does not bring him financial gain; his negotiations fail. He has to put in hard labour and suffers ill-treatment at the hands of others; he may suffer by signing documents without proper thought or scrutiny; has mental distress and also diseases arising out of imbalance of wind, bile and phlegm; sluggish liver; nervous trouble; schizophrenia etc.

Jupiter

When Jupiter is strong there is increase in wealth, learning and religious pursuits; good health; birth of a son or addition to the family; his enterprises are successful; he commands respect and receives favours from highly placed persons; his sons prosper, in female nativities, the girl may marry; if already married her husband will prosper.

But when Jupiter is weak, there may be ear-trouble, health may suffer due to improper assimilation, blood pressure *etc.*; his sons meet distress or may fall ill; there is depletion of wealth and no peace of mind. In female nativities, the husband may suffer.

Venus

When Venus is strong, the native passes a happy time; pleasures from women; increase in wealth and luxurious paraphernalia; if unmarried, the native may be married; acquisition of conveyances, gain from cattle and agriculture; travelling across the seas; success in purchase and sale of goods; gain from articles of fashion and luxury and from women; festivities, social and religious ceremonies in the family.

When Venus is weak, there is quarrel with wife; her health may suffer; diseases due to imbalance of wind and phlegm and in the region of kidney and prostrate gland or diabetes, venereal diseases; loss in purchase and sale of goods; loss in agriculture; diminution of cattle; want of cooperation from others and quarrels; waste of money on unworthy pursuits.

Saturn

When Saturn is strong the native gains from agriculture, mining, iron, oil, petrol, by employing labour, by legacy or from old persons; if in service he gets promotion and preference and holds more responsible posts; there is depth in learning and inclination for occult studies.

If Saturn is weak there is much distress of mind, loss of a relation, illness to family members, constant quarrels or litigation, labour unrest and trouble from employees; if the native himself is in employment, he may be demoted or lose job; financial loss and also loss from properties; his health may suffer from low blood pressure, nervous trouble, paralysis or ill-health due to some chronic disease; quarrels and litigation and suffering thereby.

Rahu

When Rahu is strong, there is successful travelling, promotion, increase in wealth due to transport, betting, speculation, racing, visit to a foreign country, by employing means which are not above board and by association with low people or non-Hindus.

When Rahu is weak there is depletion of wealth; the native becomes a victim of fraud or deception; demotion, transfer or travelling which causes trouble; losses in games of chance; illness due to wind trouble, skin diseases, swellings; snake-bite (if one lives in snake-infested area); company of low people and trouble thereby.

Ketu

When Ketu is strong, his period brings gain due to friendship, annihilation of enemies and daring deeds. There are religious ceremonies and visits to holy places. There is all-round increase in wealth.

But when Ketu is weak, there is trouble in the family and enmity from people; mental distress, depletion of wealth; illness to self, wife and children.

The Second Test

The second test is held on the basis of lordship of house, with the rider that if the planet is strong, during its period it shows good effects pertaining to the affairs of the house or houses of which he is the lord; on the other hand, if the planet is weak and afflicted and placed in an evil house, during its period, it shows evil effects pertaining to the matters which are judged from the house of which it is the ruler. What the matters pertaining to each house are has been discussed in Chapter IV earlier and the same is not being reiterated. How to determine whether a planet is well placed and strong or ill-placed and weak has been explained at length in Chapter VIII and those guidelines should be employed to appraise the planet.

The effects produced by a planet during its period are being divided into two paragraphs under the headings strong and weak. If the planet is strong and well placed, it will show good effects; if weak and afflicted it would mostly show evil results.

Lord of 1st

Strong: Rise in life; happiness, good health increase in wealth and status; success in undertakings.

Weak: Confinement due to illness or imprisonment; suffers from fear, sickness, mental distress; death in family; loss of wealth; enmity; misfortunes.

Lord of 2nd

Strong: Increase in family; good food; good eloquence and gain of money by speech (verbal negotiations *etc.*); happiness due to children.

Weak: Indiscretion in speech; loss of wealth; diseases of mouth and eyes; worries, misery and sorrow; death.

Lord of 3rd

Strong: Love and cooperation from brothers; happy tidings; increase in courage and valour and accomplishment of targets; occupying an eminent position; popularity.

Weak: Loss of brothers or quarrel with them; much
                   adverse criticism by others; much mental distress
                   due to enemies; defeat; disrespect to the native.

Lord of 4th

Strong: Occupying a good place; acquisition of immovable
                   property; gain of wealth and conveyances; gain
                   from agriculture; good turn from relations.

Weak: Trouble to mother; loss of property; fear from
                   water; destruction of cattle; misfortunes.

Lord of 5th

Strong: Promotion to a high government post; birth of
                   a son or happiness from children; much progress
                   in learning; respect; a happy life in company of
                   relations; virtuous conduct.

Weak: Loss of son or distress on account of children;
                   confusion of mind—taking wrong decisions or
                   loss due to indecisiveness, mental aberration;
                   loss of one's strength, virility and power;
                   disfavour from government; futile wandering;
                   becomes victim of fraud; setback in education;
                   diseases of the stomach.

Lord of 6th

Strong: Good health; generosity; increase in the number
                   of servants or subordinates; gain of wealth; is
                   not overcome by enemies; courageously crushes
                   his opponents; gets good employment;

Weak: Many evil deeds; depletion of wealth; suffers from
                   wounds and diseases; fear from thieves; is suppressed
                   or vanquished by others; if so far independent,
                   may have to work under subordination or may
                   lose employment.

Lord of 7th

Strong: Increase in luxurious paraphernalia; all kinds
                   of enjoyments particularly pleasures of the sex;

| | if unmarried, will be married; successful journey; auspicious events in house, prosperity in partnership business. |
| *Weak:* | Separation from wife/husband; distress to son-in-law; loss due to women (in female nativities due to men); disease in private part; aimless wandering; follows illegal or immoral ways; break up of partnership business or loss therein; death. |

Lord of 8th

| *Strong:* | Discharge of debts; building of a house (other than the ancestral one); elevation; increase in servants and cattle; cessation of hostilities; gain from legacy. |
| *Weak:* | Excessive sorrow; loss of equanimity of mind; envy; stupor due to imbalanced mind; diseases; poverty; disrespect; disgrace; aimless wandering. |

Lord of 9th

| *Strong:* | Devotion to gods and *brahmanas;* good and virtuous acts; religious performances; all round prosperity and increase in wealth; happiness from wife, sons and grand children, peaceful and moral enjoyment. |
| *Weak:* | Displeasure of gods and consequent suffering; distress to father, wife and children; evil deeds; death of a senior member of the family. |

Lord of 10th

| *Strong:* | Promotion; increase in respect; honour; much name and fame; clever and successful activities; increase in wealth; comfortable life; the native becomes successful in all work, he undertakes; helpful journeys. |
| *Weak:* | Loss of prestige; dishonour; improfitable journeys; evil conduct; all kinds of troubles; whatever the native undertakes ends in frustration. |

Lord of 11th

Strong: Happiness and great prosperity; increase in the number of employees; uninterrupted influx of wealth and enjoyment in the company of friends and relations.

Weak: Trouble to brother (particularly elder); distress to sons; diseases of the ear; poverty and humiliation; sorrowful tidings; the native may become a victim of fraud and deception.

Lord of 12th

Strong: Generous in spending on good causes; virtuous acts; performance of deeds of religious merit.

Weak: Waning of wealth; diseases; disgrace; all kinds of diseases; imprisonment.

The attention of the readers is invited to the basic principle that if a planet is strong on all the counts *i.e.*, well placed by sign and *navansha*, is posited in a good house and conjoined with or aspected by benefic, which are lords of good house as well, extremely good results will be felt during the planet's period. Conversely, if the planet occupies an evil house and afflicted by its location in the sign and *navansha* and conjoined with or aspected by malefics which are lords of evil houses, extremely evil results would be produced. If there are some good features and others evil, mixed results would follow. According to *Jatakadesha Marga* Chapter X, Verse 37 "Of the two kind of afflictions (*i*) situation in a good sign but in an evil house such as the eighth and (*ii*) location in an unfavourable sign but in a good house such as the eleventh, the latter is not so bad as the former." These subtle shades of influence must always be kept in mind.

The Third Test

Now we are introducing our readers to a third test. According to *Ududaya Pradeepa*—a Sanskrit work on predictive astrology abridged to *Parashari* method (Parashar was a sage, who flourished several thousand years back and is in a way deemed father of Hindu astrology), planets are divided into benefics and malefics—not on account of their natural attributes as stated in Chapter V earlier but are classified as auspicious and inauspicious exclusively on the basis of ownership of houses. Thus,

(*i*)   the lord of the first is always auspicious.

(*ii*) the lords of trines *i.e.*, the fifth and the ninth houses are auspicious; the ninth lord is more auspicious than the fifth lord.

(*iii*) the lords of the third, sixth and eleventh are inauspicious; the lord of the sixth more inauspicious than the lord of the sixth and the lord of the eleventh more inauspicious than the lord of the sixth.

(*iv*) the lords of angles *i.e.*, the 1st, 4th, 7th and 10th (since we have already discussed the lord of the first, we shall deal here with lords of 4th, 7th and 10th only) if natural benefics, are auspicious but if they become the lord of 3rd, 6th or 11th also, they become inauspicious. If the lord of an angle *i.e.*, lord of 4th, 7th and 10th is a natural malefic, he is inauspicious unless this natural malefic lord of an angle becomes the lord of a trine also, the lords of 1st, 4th, 7th and 10th are stronger in increasing order.

(*v*)   the lord of the eighth is the most inauspicious. But there are two exceptions to the above rule:

(*a*) If the lord of the eighth becomes the lord of the first also (*e.g.*, for Aries ascendant Mars becomes the lord of the first and the eighth and for Libra ascendant Venus becomes the lord of the first and the eighth), he is not inauspicious; on the other hand he is auspicious.

(*b*) The other exception is that if the Sun or the Moon is the lord of the eighth (for Sagittarius ascendant the eighth house is constituted by Cancer, lord where of is the Moon; and for Capricorn ascendant the eighth house falls on Leo, of which the Sun is the ruler) he does not become inauspicious. According to one school, if the Sun is in Leo in the eighth or

the Moon is in Cancer in the eighth, then only he
becomes fully auspicious, otherwise the Sun and the
Moon, when they are lords of the eighth are not cent
percent auspicious.

(*vi*)   the lords of the second and the twelfth are neutrals. They
are neither auspicious nor inauspicious. If the Sun or the
Moon is the lord of the second or the twelfth, he will
become auspicious if occupying a good house and/or
conjoined with a planet declared auspicious on any of
the above counts. But if the Sun or the Moon as the lord
of the second or the twelfth is conjoined with an
inauspicious planet or occupies and evil house he is
deemed inauspicious. In the case of the other five planets,
if the lord of the second or the twelfth owns another
good house he is auspicious; on the other hand, if he
owns an evil house (3rd, 6th or 11th), he is deemed
inauspicious.

Yoga Karaka

(*vii*)   We are inviting the attention of our readers to two
important astrological terms in Sanskrit (*i*) *Yoga karaka*
and (*ii*) *Maraka.*

When a planet becomes the lord of an angle as well as a
trine it is called a *yoga karaka.* It becomes wholly good and
auspicious, in fact excellent and shows very good results during
its period. Thus, for Taurus ascendant, Saturn lord of ninth and
tenth, for Cancer ascendant, Mars lord of fifth and tenth; for Leo
ascendant, Mars lord of fourth and ninth, for Libra ascendant,
Saturn lord of fourth and fifth, for Capricorn ascendant, Venus
lord of fifth and tenth and for Aquarius ascendant Venus lord
of fourth and ninth are *yoag karakas.* Of course in what
measure he would show good effects will depend upon his
placement in sign and *navansha,* position in house and other
planets with whom he is conjoined with or aspected by. But
that his period would be good is certain.

Maraka

(*viii*) *Maraka* in Sanskrit means a killer. At the outset it should be determined whether the longevity is short, medium or long and then if the period of any of the following planets synchronises with that time there may be death of the native.

(*i*) The lord the second and (*ii*) the lord of the seventh—particularly so if the lord of the 2nd or 7th is in the second or the seventh house. It must be noted that if the Moon, Mercury, Venus or Jupiter is the lord of the seventh house—the planet's intensity to become a *maraka* (killer) increases in the above order. Thus, Mercury as lord of the seventh is a more potential killer than the Moon; Venus as the lord of the seventh has more *maraka* propensities than Mercury and Jupiter as lord of the seventh is the most potent killer—particularly if any of the four planets specified above occupies the second or the seventh house. But when on examination of the birth chart, the longevity is long the native may fall ill during the period of a *maraka* in the sub-period of a *maraka* or an inauspicious planet, but he does not die. If there is no period of *maraka* at the appropriate time, the native may die during the period of the lord of the 12th, 11th, 8th, 6th or the 3rd. Of all these, Saturn has the greatest propensity to kill if he is a *maraka* or lord of the 3rd, 6th or 11th. To determine the exact time of death necessitates detailed calculations which are too elaborate and complex to be laid down here and we have provided here only a bird's eye view of the principles.

Key Planets

Now we are giving key-planets, as auspicious and inauspicious for each ascendant. If the chart under examination has Aries ascendant (rising sign called *lagnam* in Sanskrit) look below under Aries. If your birth chart has Leo in the first house, look to Leo. And so on.

Aries

The Sun, Moon, Mars and Jupiter are auspicious; Mercury, Venus and Saturn are inauspicious.

Taurus

The Sun, Venus and Saturn are auspicious. Mercury is also auspicious but he can kill also due to ownership of the second house. The Moon, Mars and Jupiter are inauspicious.

Gemini

Mercury and Venus are auspicious. Jupiter (except that he has also propensity to kill) is also auspicious. The Moon is neutral and would not kill unless he is conjoined with a malefic. The Sun, Mars and Saturn are inauspicious. Saturn's ownership of the eighth outweighs his rulership of the ninth. But if Saturn is in eighth or ninth, he becomes auspicious.

Cancer

The Moon, Mars and Jupiter are auspicious. Jupiter's ruling the ninth house is more weighty than his owning the sixth. The Sun is neutral. Mercury, Venus and Saturn are inauspicious.

Leo

The Sun and Mars are auspicious. Jupiter if in fifth or eighth in his own sign is auspicious, otherwise he will show mixed results. The Moon is neutral. Mercury, Venus and Saturn are inauspicious.

Virgo

Mercury and Venus are auspicious but Venus has also propensity to kill. Jupiter also shows auspicious results but he has also propensity to kill. Saturn shows mixed results but becomes auspicious if he tenants the fifth. The Sun is neutral. The Moon and Mars are inauspicious.

Libra

Mercury, Venus, and Saturn are auspicious. The Moon is also so, but in a lesser measure. The Sun and Jupiter are inauspicious.

Scorpio

The Sun, the Moon, Mars and Jupiter are auspicious but Jupiter has also propensity to kill. Mercury, Venus and Saturn are inauspicious.

Sagittarius

The Sun, Mars and Jupiter are auspicious. Mercury is also auspicious but has propensity to kill. Venus and Saturn are inauspicious. The Moon if with eight or more digits shows good results.

Capricorn

Venus and Saturn are auspicious; Mercury is also so. His ownership of the ninth out weighs his ownership of the sixth. The Sun if placed well by sign and house is auspicious. The Moon, Mars and Jupiter are inauspicious.

Aquarius

Venus and Saturn are auspicious. The Moon, the Sun, Mars and Jupiter are inauspicious. Mercury if in the fifth or eighth shows good results. Otherwise he shows mixed results.

Pisces

The Moon, Mars and Jupiter are auspicious. Mercury is also auspicious but has propensity to kill. The Sun, Venus and Saturn are inauspicious.

If in the above classification, the lord of the third is in third or the lord of the sixth in sixth or the lord of the eleventh in eleventh, he is not deemed inauspicious but shows good results during his period.

While judging an individual horoscope, it should be borne in mind that if the lord of a trine has sambandh with the lord of an angle, it causes very good results during the periods of the planets (lords of the angle and trine having *sambandha*).

It would be an excellent testimony for *raja-yoga* if the lord of an angle has *sambandha* with the lords of both the trines or if the lord of a trine has *sambandha* with the lords of more than one angle.

The result is not so good if the above lords of an angle and a trine have simultaneously *sambandha* with the lord of the third, sixth, eighth or eleventh.

But suppose the lord of the trine is also the lord of a bad house or the lord of an angle along with his rulership of an angle has the lordship of an evil house also, even then, a *sambandha* between the lords of a trine and an angle is good and during their periods good results follow. Of course, if they (along with lordships of trine and angle) had not been lords of unfavourable houses, it would have been par excellence.

Rahu posited in an angle and conjoined with the lord of a trine or posited in a trine and conjoined with the lord of an angle gives very good results. The above principle enunciated in regard to Rahu also applies to Ketu.

All planets, when their periods are current have a tendency to cause some depression in matters governed by the house, which has the planet's sign of debilitation thereon. And the planet during his period elevates the affairs of the house where his sign of exaltation falls. For example suppose Leo is the ascendant and the Sun's period is current; since Libra the sign of Sun's debilitation falls on the third house its affairs will suffer. And because Aries where the Sun (lord of the period) is exalted, falls in the ninth house, the affairs of this house will prosper.

We have provided enough guidelines for assessment of periods of planets and readers will acquire insight and discrimination in increasing measure as they examine larger and larger number of birth charts and compare their assessment with the actual trends in life and events in the lives of persons, whose birth charts have been so scrutinised by them.

Now we shall pass on to the sub-periods.

Sub-Periods

Periods of planets extend to many years. Venus continues for twenty years; Saturn for nineteen. Even the shortest—that of the Sun—covers six years. It is true, some persons go on having continuous meteoric rise; others go on declining in wealth and career and many continue a humdrum life. Still, in most cases we find that the river of life does not flow evenly.

The long period of Venus extending to twenty years or that of Jupiter covering sixteen, will at times be very good, at others ordinary and at yet others very unfavourable and trying. Sometimes, the effects may not be felt on the same plane. The native may continue to be rich but his health may suffer or he may lose in litigation or a family member may fall seriously ill or even die. Sometimes, there is no overt act which may be called evil but despite wealth and position, he may suffer from intense anguish of mind. And thus the even tenure of life is disturbed. It is, therefore, to facilitate this enquiry of favourable and unfavourable times, that the system of sub-periods in a period has been improvised. How to calculate the sub-periods in a period has been explained in the preceding chapter. To narrow down the scope of the period, we take recourse to sub-periods. And to further pin-point this time we take into consideration the transits. Transits have been dealt with in detail in the succeding chapter, so here we shall limit our observations to sub-periods only.

General Principles

1. Judge the lord of the sub-period in the same manner as we have laid down for judging the lord of the period. Apply all the three tests prescribed earlier, and after weighing the favourable and unfavourable factors determine whether the lord of the sub-period is strong or weak, auspicious or inauspicious. And the rules in regard to the effects of period should *mutatis mutandis* be applied to sub-periods also.

2. When the period is good and the sub-period is also good, there is all round happiness, progress, prosperity and good time.

3. When the period and the sub-period are both evil they would bring misery to the native. Whether it will be poverty, illness, death, trouble from enemies, loss in litigation, domestic misery or any other kind of evil must be ascertained from the planets whose period and sub-period are current. A planet, apart from its inherent nature

shows the effect of the house or houses of which it is the lord, the house it is posited in and aspects, the planets it is conjoined with or aspected by. This applies to good effects also—as to what type of good effect will be felt.

4. When the period is good and the sub-period evil, mostly the evil effects of the sub-period predominate but due to the goodness of the period, the evil effects do not go to extremes. For example, if one is running the period of a *yoga karaka*, even the sub-period of a *maraka* will not kill the native; he may only fall seriously ill.

5. When the period is evil and the sub-period good, favourable results will be had, but the good will not be in marked measure, because the evil nature of the period would act as a dragging down weight.

6. If the sub-period lord is in the sixth, eighth or twelfth from the period lord, there is much struggle. If both are evil, extremely evil results would follow. If both are *marakas*, and the general examination of the horoscope shows that longevity must come to an end the native may even die.

7. When the sub-period lord is in twelfth from the period lord, there is heavy expenditure.

8. A planet whose period is current does not show its full effect during its own sub-period in its period. The full effect of this period lord is felt during the sub-period of the planet who is of a similar nature as the period lord or has *sambandha* with the period lord. What do we mean by two planets being of a similar nature ? It means that if according to the third test laid down on pages 129—130, both the planets are auspicious then they would be deemed to be of similar nature; if both the planets are inauspicious then also they would be deemed to be of a similar nature.

9. Venus and Saturn have a special disposition in regard to effects produced during one's sub-period in the period of the other. When the period of Venus is current, the effect of Venus will be felt in the sub-period of Saturn. In

the period of Venus, his own sub-period, the effects of Saturn will be felt. Similarly, when the period of Saturn is current, Saturn will show his effect in the sub-period of Venus. In Saturn's period—during his own sub-period, the effects of Venus would come to pass. This special disposition of Venus and Saturn is confined to the periods of these two planets only and to the sub-periods of these two planets therein.

10. (*a*) When there is the period of planet which is the lord of an angle and the sub-period of a planet which is the lord of a trine or (*b*) when there is the period of a planet which is the lord of a trine and the sub-period of the lord of an angle, the sub-period produces very good results if there is a *sambandha* between the lords of the angle and the trine whose period and sub-periods are current. Further during the period of planet (which if lord of an angle has *sambandha* with the lord of a trine, or if lord of a trine has *sambandha* with the lord of an angle) there is good luck and prosperity even during the sub-periods of other auspicious planets.

11. Saturn has greater propensity than any other planet to kill. This means that if the period of a planet, which is likely to kill, is current, Saturn's sub-period therein is likely to prove fatal. Similarly, when Saturn's period is current in old age, the native is likely to die in one of the sub-periods of a *maraka*, because as stated earlier, the full effect of a planet is not felt in its own sub-period in its period.

12. A *maraka* planet does not kill, when its period is current, during the sub-period of an auspicious planet, though this auspicious planet has *sambandha* with the *maraka* planet. The *maraka* planet, when its period is current kills during the sub-period of an inauspicious planet though the lords of the period and sub-period have no *sambandha*.

13. The sub-period lord has a tendency to precipitate the event—whether good or evil—which depends upon

whether the sub-period lord is auspicious—when the
Sun transits the sign owned by the sub-period lord.
Thus, if we have to fix the solar month during which
Mars as sub-period lord would precipitate the event
look up the ephemeris to find during which dates the
Sun would transit Aries and Scorpio—the two signs
owned by Mars. The effect of Mars will be more
intensely felt during the two solar months specified
above. If suppose we have to find when Jupiter as
lord of the sub-period would confer results, look-up
the ephemeris and see when the Sun transits Sagittarius
and Pisces—the two signs owned by Jupiter. The
results are more likely during the Sun's transit through
these two signs and so on.

Rough and Ready Methods

We are now providing some rough and ready methods which
obviate the necessity of calculating the periods and sub-periods.

Age	Planet
(*i*) birth to 4 years	The Moon rules.
(*ii*) 5th to 14th	Mercury has sway.
(*iii*) 15th to 22nd	Venus presides.
(*iv*) 23rd to 41st	The Sun has control.
(*v*) 42nd to 56th	Mars rules.
(*vi*) 57th to 68th	Jupiter has sway.
(*vii*) From 69th onwards	Saturn dominates.

Thus, suppose a person aged 39 comes to you and you find
that in his chart the Sun is very afflicted and Mars very strong,
you may safely say that his miseries would end with his 41st
year and he will have very good time from 42nd to 56th year.
These planetary periods apply to all people. You have merely
to look at the birth chart and predict good period (as given
above) if the presiding planet is auspicious and strong. If
the planet having control, according to the above table is
weak and inauspicious, you have to say that the particular
period would be unfavourable.

Another Method

The following year of age are allotted to planets: Sun 22; Moon 24; Mars 28; Mercury 32; Jupiter 16; Venus 25; Saturn 36; Rahu 42; Ketu 48.

Suppose the native comes to you in his 20th year and asks you when he would get into employment and you find the Sun is in Leo in the tenth, you may safely say that he would have a good job in his 22nd year. But suppose the sun is weak and afflicted in his horoscope then his 22nd year will be unfavourable.

Take another example. A girl comes to you in her twenty-third year. You find that in her chart the Moon is the owner of a good house and posited in the seventh and aspected by Jupiter. You may safely predict that she would be married in her twenty-fourth year, because the Moon is in the seventh-house of marriage and well aspected and the Moon's year is 24th.

There is yet another way to utilise the significance of these years. Suppose the Sun is the lord of the ninth house and well-placed anywhere in the chart. Since ninth is the house of good luck you say that the native's 22nd year would be a good one. Take another example. Suppose Capricorn is the rising sign then the Moon would be ruler of the seventh house. Now, if the Moon is well-placed anywhere in the chart then you may predict marriage in the 24th year.

Houses and Years

Now we are dealing with another method. We are stating below an analogy between years of age and the houses in the birth chart.

House	Years of Age
IX house	1st to 24th
X "	25th and 26th
XI "	27th and 28th
XII "	29th and 30th
I "	31st to 33rd
II "	34th to 36th
III "	37th to 39th
IV "	40th to 45th
V "	46th to 51st
VI "	52nd to 57th
VII "	58th to 65th
VIII "	66th year onwards.

Suppose a person comes to you in his 38th year. On examining his birth chart you find that planets in the third house are weak and afflicted and the lord of the fourth is strong in fourth and beneficially aspected—you may safely predict that his troubles will come to an end when his 39th year is complete and the period from 40th to 45th year will be a good one. Before we close this chapter, we would like to add that throughout the last so many centuries, it has been confirmed by experience that if a planet is adverse in the birth chart, the best way to mitigate its evil influence is to wear the gem prescribed for it. Please refer to pages 48-49. It is always better to put on the gem for a trial period of three days and if it shows good results during the period, it should be worn permanently—studded in a ring or a locket, so that the lower surface is in direct contact with the skin and the upper surface exposed to the atmosphere. If, say a particular piece of blue sapphire does not suit you and shows some adverse effect during the trial period, discard it at once, And then try another piece of blue sapphire after a few days. The metals worn next to the skin also alleviate the suffering caused by the planets but not in that measure as the gems. If a planet is not adverse in your birth chart, and even then if you put on the gem, it would further enhance the good effects. So putting on of suitable gems is always good. This gem therapy applies not only to the radical positions of planets in your birth chart but to planetary periods, sub-periods and transits as well.

CHAPTER XI

TRANSITS

In a large number of horoscopes, the bare chart is provided, without longitudes of planets or planetary periods and sub-periods. For such a contingency, a rough and ready method for timing events, is being provided. And even while making predictions on the basis of a fully worked out chart, a consideration of the transits is essential for arriving at accurate predictions—though it must be emphasised that the influences of the planetary periods and sub-periods are primary, while those of the transits are secondary.

What is a transit ? In astrology, it means the passing of a planet through a particular part of the zodiac *i.e.*, through a particular sign. The birth chart is fixed and static. The position of planets in the birth chart gives the location of the planets as they were at the time of birth. But the planets are not stationary; they are always going round in their orbits. So, when we take into consideration the effects of transits, what we actually do is to take into account, wherein their respective passages, the various planets are in the heavens at the time for which transits are being considered. Suppose you have to judge the effects of transits for December, 1976 then you must have the ephemeris for 1976 with you to mark where the planets would be in that year. Here, again, it is reiterated that Hindu astrology being sidereal, you must have an ephemeris computed for the sidereal zodiac such as Lahiri's Indian Ephemeris. If you have an ephemeris furnishing longitudes of planets in the tropical zodiac such as Raphael's, the precession of the equinoxes for that year must be deducted from the tropical longitudes, to arrive at the sidereal longitudes. If you ignore this, your judgment in regard to transits may well be off the mark.

In Hindu astrology, transits are judged generally from the moonsign. What is the moonsign ? The sign in which the Moon was at the time of birth. In the example horoscope worked out in Chapter II, the Moon is in Sagittarius. So the moonsign in this horoscope is Sagittarius. Suppose, your Moon at birth was in Pisces. Then your moonsign is Pisces. Now, when we say Mars by transit in the eighth, it should mean Mars in Libra, because Libra would be eighth from Pisces. Suppose your friend's Moon at birth was in Cancer. Then his moonsign would be Cancer, When we say Saturn by transit in the third, it would mean Saturn travelling through Virgo, because Virgo is third from Cancer. And so on.

So, all references to first, second, third *etc.,* in this chapter must be counted from the moonsign of the person, whose chart is under consideration.

In India, the Moonsign is commonly referred to as *janma-rashi* or just *rashi.* This Sanskrit word *rashi* literally means a sign, but by extended meaning it connotes the sign in which the moon was at birth. In English, the Moon at birth is referred to as the radical Moon. When we have to refer to any planet as in the birth chart *i.e.,* at the time of birth, to indicate this we add radical *e.g.* the radical Sun, the radical Mars, the radical Mercury *etc.* And when we have to refer to the position at the time of the transit, we say the transiting Sun, the transiting Moon, the transiting Mars and so on. Suppose a person has the Moon in Scorpio in the birth chart and on the day he consults an astrologer, the Moon is in Gemini. Then we say 'the transiting Moon is the eighth from the radical Moon', because Gemini would be eighth from Scorpio. For those who are acquainted with the astrological terminology, all this would appear superfluous, but the needs of the beginners have also to be kept in mind and every step—every terminology is being explained at length, to make the path of comprehension easier.

Transits of the Sun

As counted from the radical Moon, when the Sun transits.

(*i*) 3rd, 6th, 10th and 11th, he shows good results.

(*ii*) 1st, 2nd, 5th, 7th and 9th, he is unfavourable.

(*iii*) 4th, 8th and 12th, he is evil.

But when the Sun transits some places from the radical Moon, and if a planet, other than Saturn, is transiting a sensitive area the effects of the Sun's transit are obstructed. In astrological mythology, the Sun is the father of Saturn and so except for Saturn's transit, any other planet or planets in the sensitive area would neutralize the good or bad effects,

These sensitive areas or obstructing places are called *vedha* in Sanskrit.

Vedha

3	6	10	11
9	12	4	5

(*i*) 3 and 9, (*ii*) 6 and 12, (*iii*) 10 and 4 and (*iv*) 11 and 5 constitute four pairs. If the Sun is transiting 3rd from the radical Moon and any planet (other than Saturn) is simultaneously transiting 9th from the radical Moon, the Sun's influence would be obstructed. Conversely, if the Sun is transiting the 9th from the radical Moon and any planet other than Saturn is transiting the 3rd from the radical Moon the Sun's influence would be obstructed. And so on.

Transits of Moon

The Moon completes one orbit—covering all the twelve signs—in about 27 days. So he is in one sign for 2 days and 6 hours approximately. When judging the transits of the Moon, we have to find which sign he is passing through—as counted from the moonsign at birth.

(*i*) The transiting Moon is favourable when he transits 1st, 2nd, 3rd, 5th, 6th, 7th, 9th, 10th and 11th as counted from the radical Moon.

(*ii*) The transiting Moon is evil when he is going through the 4th, 8th and 12th as counted from the birth moonsign.

Vedha

1	3	6	7	10	11
5	9	12	2	4	8

When the transiting Moon is in 1st (from the radical Moon) his influence is obstructed if a planet other than Mercury is at the time transiting the

5th from the radical Moon. In astrological mythology the Moon had liaison with Jupiter's wife Tara and as a result Mercury was born. So, we have stated that any planet other than Mercury will obstruct the influence of the Moon because the son (Mercury) does not obstruct the effects generated by the father (Moon). It would be clear from the above table that (*i*) 1 and 5, (*ii*) 3 and 9, (*iii*) 6 and 12, (*iv*) 7 and 2, (*v*) 10 and 4 and (*iv*) 11 and 8 are the mutually corresponding places. To illustrate, when the transiting Moon is in 8th his influence will be obstructed by a planet, other than Mercury transiting the 11th from the radical Moon. Conversely, when the transiting Moon is in 11th from his radical position and any planet other than Mercury by transit in 8th from the radical Moon the good effects will be under check.

Transits of Mars

As counted from the radical Moon, when Mars transits

(*i*) 3rd, 6th, 10th and 11th, he is very favourable.
(*ii*) 1st, 2nd, 5th, 7th and 9th, he is unfavourable.
(*iii*) 4th, 8th, and 12th, he is evil.

Vedha

3	6	11
12	9	5

(*i*) When Mars is in 3rd, any planet in 12th, (*ii*) when Mars is in 12th any planet in 3rd, (*iii*) when Mars is in 6th any planet in 9th, (*iv*) when Mars is in 9th any planet in 6th, (*v*) when Mars is in 11th any planet in 5th and (*vi*) when Mars is in 5th any planet in 11th will keep Mars' influence—favourable or unfavourable as the case may be—under check. The count is always to be made from the moonsign at birth.

Transits of Mercury

From the radical Moon when Mercury transits

(*i*) 2nd, 6th, 10th, and 11th, he is very favourable.
(*ii*). 1st, 3rd, 5th, 7th, and 9th, he is unfavourable.
(*iii*) 4th, 8th and 12th, he is evil.

Vedha

2	4	6	8	10	11
5	3	9	1	8	12

To illustrate, Mercury in 2nd from the radical Moon is obstructed by a planet other than the transiting Moon in the 5th from the radical Moon and vice versa. As Mercury and Moon are son and father, Mercury's influence is obstructed by any transiting planet, except the transiting Moon. The father and the son do not obstruct each other's influence. The count is always to be made from the radical Moon (moonsign in the birth chart).

Transits of Jupiter

From the radical Moon when Jupiter transits

(*i*) 2nd, 5th, 7th, 9th and 11th, he is very favourable.
(*ii*) 1st, 3rd, 6th, and 10th, he is unfavourable.
(*iii*) 4th, 8th and 12th, he is evil.

Vedha

2	5	7	9	11
12	4	3	10	8

Thus, Jupiter by transit in 2nd from the radical Moon will not show good effect when any planet is transiting the 12th from the radical Moon. Conversely Jupiter in 12th from the moonsign at birth will not show evil effect, when any planet is transiting 2nd from the radical Moon.

TRANSITS OF VENUS

From the radical Moon when Venus transits

(*i*) 1st, 2nd, 3rd, 9th and 11th, he is very favourable.
(*ii*) 5th, 6th, 7th, and 10th, he is unfavourable.
(*iii*) 4th, 8th and 12th, he is evil.

Vedha

1	2	3	4	5	8	9	11	12
8	7	1	10	9	5	11	6	3

The corresponding places are 1 and 8; 2 and 7; 3 and 1 and so on. So when Venus is transiting the 1st from the radical Moon, any planet in 8th from the radical Moon would obstruct his influence and so on.

Transits of Saturn

From the radical Moon when Saturn transits

(*i*) 3rd, 6th, 10th, and 11th, he is favourable.
(*ii*) 1st, 2nd, 5th, 7th and 9th, he is unfavourable.
(*iii*) 4th, 8th and 12th, he is evil.

Vedha

3	6	11
12	9	5

Thus, when Saturn is transiting the 3rd from the radical Moon, if any planet other than the Sun is transiting the 12th from the radical Moon, Saturn's influence would be kept under check. Conversely, when Saturn transits the 12th (from the moonsign at birth) if any planet other than the Sun transits the 3rd (from the moonsign at birth) Saturn's influence would be obstructed. So in the case of other pairs (*i*) 6 and 9 and (*ii*) 11 and 5. The Sun and Saturn being father and son do not obstruct each other's influence.

Transits of Rahu and Ketu

The transits of Rahu and Ketu should be treated in the same way as those of Saturn with the diffference that the Sun, does not act as an obstructing force in case of Saturn, but does so in case of Rahu or Ketu. Rahu and Ketu are always in seventh from each other, so Rahu does not act as an obstructing factor for Ketu nor Ketu for Rahu.

General Principle

The particulars of good and evil transits given in the preceding pages in this chapter merely provide mathematical tables, whithout overriding rules for individual appreciation. We shall therefore lay down some guidelines below:

In our opinion the readers may omit from their consideration—all that has been stated about *vedha i.e.* obstruction of the influence of the transit, for even ancient authorties are divided on the point[1]. Their inferences from transits would be more correct if they pay attention to the following rules instead:

1. Planets when transiting the 12th from the radical Moon or from the birth ascendant cause heavy expenditure, particularly so when two or three planets are simultaneously transiting the 12th (from the ascendant or the radical Moon). Malefics in particular,cause not only expenses but losses as well.

---

1. See excerpts from *Narad, Kashyap Mandavya, Vashishtha, Brihaspati* etc. given by the Sanskrit Commentary Piyush Dhara on Muhoorta Chintamani.

2. The Sun, Mercury and Venus cover their transits through the twelve signs during one year. These planets stay in a sign for about a month or so. Readers will do well to make a survey of their past years and arrive at conclusions, as to which months agree with them better. One relevant point has, however, to be noted in this connection. The solar months and the calendar months are not identical. The solar month begins when the Sun enters a sign and ends when he steps into the next one. The exact dates of entries of planets in various signs and how long each planet would stay in one sign, can be known from the current ephemeris.

3. (*i*) If a planet is strong by sign in your birth chart and well-placed in house—particularly if it be in the 3rd,6th, 10th or 11th from the birth ascendant or the radical Moon in your birth chart, it does not show very bad results even when it is transiting an unfavourable house.

(*ii*) The same is the case when the planet (whose transit is under consideration) is the owner of good houses or a *yoga karaka* in your birth chart.

4. If a planet is strong by sign and house in your birth chart and particularly in the 3rd, 6th, 10th or 11th from your birth ascendant or the radical Moon, it shows very good results when it is transiting favourable houses.

5. If a planet is weak (in sign and *navansha* of debilitation or in a sign and *navansha* owned by an enemy or great enemy) and, conjoined with or aspected by malefics and not conjoined with benefics or aspected by them and owner of evil houses in the birth chart particularly so, if it rules evil houses counted both from the birth ascendant and the radical Moon, it does not show appreciably good results, even when it is transiting favourable houses.

6. (*i*) During the course of transit, if a planet is conjoined with or aspected by malefics, its propensity to do good is reduced and its power to do evil is enhanced.

(*ii*) The same is the case when a planet becomes combust or transits its sign of debilitation or *navansha* in which it would be debilitated.

7. (*i*) During the transit, when a planet is conjoined with
    or aspected by benefics, its power to do good is enhanced
    and the propensity to do evil is mitigated.

    (*ii*) The same is the case when it is transiting its own sign or
    sign of exaltation or own *navansha* or a *navansha* in
    which it would be exalted.

8. Benefic become more powerful for the good when
    they become retrograde during the transit. Malefic
    become more malignant to do evil. when during their
    transit they turn retrograde.

9. The maximum effect—benefic or malefic—is felt when
    two or more planet during transit generate similar effect
    (good or evil).

10. In short, the condition (location in sign and house from
    the birth ascendant as well as from the radical Moon) of
    the transiting planet should be judged not only during
    the transit but in the birth chart as well.

11. Malefics transiting unfavourable houses—show more
    malefic influence, if the sign transited is occupied by
    planets in your birth chart and particularly so if the
    transiting planet has very slow motion during transit.[1]

12. Benefics transiting signs—show much more benefic effect
    if the sign—transited is occupied by planets in your
    birth chart, particularly so if the transiting planet has
    very slow motion during transit.

13. If a sign is beneficially aspected in your birth chart,
    even malefics would not be so malignant during transit
    through the sign and the transits of benefics would be
    better. Conversely, if the sign receives malefic aspects
    in your birth chart, transits of even benefics would not
    be so good and transits of malefics would be worse.

---

1. The Sun's motion does not vary very much. The Moon's average motion
   is 13°—10' per day the Mercury and Venus cover the zodiac in one
   year, so they may be treated as fast when their motion is more then 59-8'
   per day. The average motion of Mars may be taken as 33'-28" per day,
   that of Jupiter 5' daily and of Saturn 2'. Rahu and Ketu have uniform
   motion of 3'-11".

14. The transit of a planet posited in the ascendant in your birth chart, during its transit through the twelve houses— shows the effect of the house (from the ascendant) it is transiting.

15. Whatever good or bad a planet shows in the birth chart will be felt when the planet transits the ascendant.

16. During transit the Sun and Mars show marked effect when they transit 0° to 10° in the sign; Jupiter and Venus generate their influence more effectively when they are in the middle of the sign (10° to 20°) and the Moon and Saturn during their transit through the last ten degrees of the sign. Mercury, Rahu and Ketu exert their influence throughout (0° to 30°).

17. The type of good or bad effect generated by a planet during transit depends upon its ownership and location in the birth chart as well as the matters it is a significator for and also which house it is transiting as counted from the (*i*) radical Moon, (*ii*) his own radical position in the birth chart and (*iii*) from the birth ascendant. For significance of houses and planets, the readers are referred to earlier chapters.

We have in this book provided enough guidelines. To appraise the birth chart—the various departments of life and to judge timings of events on the basis of the planetary periods and sub-periods, as well as from transits and request the readers to examine their own birth chart and the birth charts of their friends and acquaintances to gain practical experience. The various influences at work some time apparently contradictory— have to by synthesised and the resultant arrived at. And that can be done only be practice. Be it astrology or any other science, no theoretical knowledge alone will enable you to master the subject. Practice alone makes one perfect, and experience is the best instructor.

TABLE OF PRECESSION OF EQUINOXES AND NUTATION

Below is being given the table of precession of equinoxes and nutation on the 1st of January of every alternate year from 1900 to 1974. The value for any date in between can be calculated by rule of three and then rounded off to the nearest minute.

Year	D. M. S.	Year	D. M. S.
1900	22 28 5	1938	22 59 50
1902	22 29 39	1940	23 1 23
1904	22 31 8	1942	23 2 54
1906	22 32 38	1944	23 4 23
1908	22 34 12	1946	23 6 0
1910	22 35 54	1948	23 7 44
1912	22 37 42	1950	23 9 35
1914	22 39 34	1952	23 11 25
1916	22 41 24	1954	23 13 15
1918	22 43 8	1956	23 14 56
1920	22 44 45	1958	23 16 31
1922	22 46 16	1960	23 17 55
1924	22 47 44	1962	23 19 24
1926	22 49 17	1964	23 20 59
1928	22 50 56	1966	23 22 41
1930	22 52 43	1968	23 24 30
1932	22 54 33	1970	23 26 21
1934	22 56 25	1972	23 28 11
1936	22 58 11	1974	23 29 55

AYANAMSA

Year	Ayanamsa		Year	Ayanamsa	
1976	23	31.3	2004	23	54.8
1978	23	33.0	2006	23	56.4
1980	23	34.7	2008	23	58.1
1982	23	36.3	2010	23	59.8
1984	23	38.0	2012	24	01.5
1986	23	39.7	2014	24	03.1
1988	23	41.4	2016	24	04.8
1990	23	43.0	2018	24	06.5
1992	23	44.7	2020	24	08.2
1994	23	46.4	2022	24	09.8
1996	23	48.1	2024	24	11.5
1998	23	49.7	2026	24	13.2
2000	23	51.4	2028	24	14.9
2002	23	53.1	2030	24	16.6
			2032	24	18.2

Motion for Ayanamsa :

10 years	00	08.38
100 years	01	23.8

SANSKRIT WORDS

Antardasha (103)* : Sub-periods of Planets; antar.

Apoklim (36) : Cadent. The 3rd, 6th, 9th, and 12th, houses. Planets in these houses show delayed effects.

Ashtottari (103) : One of the 53 kinds of Mahadashas. The duration of the total cycle of this mahadasha is 108 years. This is used in Bengal and Western India (Gujarat in particular).

Ayurveda (91) : The Ancient system of Medicine in India. This is based on the three humours *viz.*, Vata (wind), Pitta (bile), and Kapha (phelgm). The imbalance of these tri-doshas (one, two, or all the three) causes most health disorders. The treatment is done through Herbs, different kinds of oils, and medicines made out of precious jewels.

Basti (29) : The portion of stomach between the navel and genitals (excluding it) when divided in two parts, then the lower portion is called Basti and falls under Libra.

---

* Numbers given in the brackets after each Sanskrit word indicate the page number on which it appears.

Bhagya (39)	: Fortunes, good luck.
Bhukti (103)	: In Southern India Antardashas or sub-periods of planets are called Bhukti.
Brihaspati (7)	: The planet Jupiter. The greater Fortuna. Generally a benefic. It is also the name of the Guru of the Gods (Devtas).
Budh (7)	: Mercury. Rules the mind, logic and discriminations; has two sides—Good Mercury creates orators, writers, actors and inventors. It also has a negative side when it makes one a confidence trickster, undependable and crooked. Mercury in Cancer and Pisces can cause lower I.Q. in the family.
Chandra (7)	: Moon. Rules emotions in men and health in women; indicates mass popularity when strong. Imparts sensitivity and maternal touch.
Dashas (103)	: Periods of planets. Mahadashas or Major periods of planets. It is calculated on the basis of the Longitude of Moon in the Sidereal horoscope.
Dhanu (6)	: Sagittarius. Ruled by Jupiter; when this sign is prominent in a horoscope, it makes one restless, jovial, and ambitious.
Graha (7)	: Planets.
Guru (7)	: Jupiter or Brihaspati. Brihaspati (Rishi) is the name of the Guru of Devtas (Gods).
Janmarashi (88)	: The sign occupied by Moon at birth. It is of great significance as transits of planets are judged from the Janmarashi. In India the first alphabet

of the name corresponded to the janmarashi *i.e.*, the quarter of the Janma nakshatra that the Moon occupied in the Janmarashi.

Kanya (6) : Virgo; ruled by Mercury.

Kapha (91) : One of the three humours in Ayurveda, Phelgm.

Karaka (98) : Significator; A planet who has jurisdiction on a living being or element *viz.*, Sun signifies father, Atma (soul), the first house etc.

Karka (6) Cancer. Movable. Water.

Kendra (56) : Angles. The 1st, 4th, 7th, and the 10th house is called an angle.

Ketu (7) : The southern node of Moon. The 9th planet in Hindu Astrology. Similar to Mars in nature. 'Cauda Draconis'.

Kuja (7) : Mars; Mangal.

Kumbha (6) : Aquarius. Ruled by Saturn.

Lagnam (22) : Ascendant. The Rising sign. The first house of the horoscope.

Mahadashas (103) : Major periods of planets. Also called Dashas in short.

Makara (6) : Capricorn. Ruled by Saturn.

Mangala (7) : Mars.

Maraka (55, 125) : The ruler of the 2nd or 7th house.

Meena (6) : Pisces. Ruled by Jupiter.

Mesha (6) : Aries. Ruled by Mars.

Mithuna (6) : Gemini. Ruled by Mercury.

Moolatrikona (41) : A certain position where a planet is endowed with extra strength as compared to its position in own sign. The degrees between which they are in their Moolatrikona are mentioned at the page no 41.

Nakshatras (4) : Constellation. The twenty-seven

fixed stars *viz.,* Ashwini, Bharani, Krittika etc. are called Nakshatras. The Zodiac divided into 27 parts, each consisting of 13 degrees and 20 minutes, are given the names of the above fixed stars in order.

Navansha (32)   : A sign of 30 degrees divided into nine parts of 3 degrees and 20 minutes, is called a navansha (one by nine portion). The strength of a planet in the navansha is significant similar to (even more) its strength in the birth chart.

Panaphara (36)   : Succeedent. The 2nd, 5th, 8th, 11th, houses. Planets in these houses show effect in the middle portion of life or in the middle period of their Dashas.

Pitta (91)   : The second of the three Humours *viz.,* bile.

Pratyantara (104)   : Subdivisions of the sub-periods (of a mahadasha) into nine smaller periods.

Rahu (6)   : The northern node of the Moon; Caput Draconis.

Raja Yoga (99)   : A position of or a combination of one, two or more Planets in the birth chart which lifts the native to a high position of exaltation in life. It is formed when the lord of an angle and the lord of a trine develops a 'Sambandh'. At times a single planet all alone confers it. If more than two planets combine then the strength increases manifolds.

Rashi (32)   : Sign. A division of Zodiac in twelve parts. The sign teneted by Moon at

	birth is also called in short "Rashi".
Ravi (7)	: Sun. Ruler of Leo.
Sambandha (91)	: A relationship between two planets (for details see page 91)
Shani (7)	: Saturn. Ruler of Capricorn and Aquarius.
Shukra (7)	: Venus. The lesser Fortuna. Rules Taurus and Libra.
Simha (6)	: Leo. Ruled by Sun. The fifth sign in the Zodiac.
Surya (7)	: Ravi; Sun.
Tribaghi (103)	: One of the kinds of Mahadashas; The cycle (duration) of this is eighty years. It is mostly used in Nepal (the only Hindu country in the north of India and in the Valleys of Himalayas).
Trik (36)	: The three evil ones *viz.*, the 6th, 8th, and 12th houses together are called 'Trik'. Planets in these show bad results. Out of the three, the 8th is the worst known as the Chidrasthana or Shoonya (Zero).
Trikona (36)	: The Trine. The 5th, 9th, and the 1st are called Trikona. The 1st is both an angle and a Trikona.
Tula (6)	: Libra. Ruled by Venus. The 7th Sign in the Zodiac.
Upachaya (36)	: Its meaning is 'increase'. The 3rd, 6th, 10th and 11th houses are called Upachaya. Malefics in these houses show good results.
Vargottam (47)	: When a planet or Ascendant is in the same sign (rashi) in the Birth chart as well as in the Navansha chart then it is called vargottam. The effect of such a planet is extraordinary to do good.

Vata (91)   : Vayu. The first humour in Ayurveda: 'wind'.

Vedha (137)   : Obstruction of or barring the influence of a planet in transit. The transit is taken from the Janmarashi (Moon-Sign).

Vinsbottari (or Vimshottari) (103) : One of 53 types of periods of planets; widely used all over India. This is the most popular of the dashas and has a total cycle of 120 years.

Vrisha: Taurus (6) : Ruled by Venus. The second sign in the Zodiac.

Vrischik (6)   : Scorpio. Ruled by Mars. The 8th sign in the Zodiac.

Yoga (99)   : A combination or addition of two and more factors.

Yoga Karka (124) : A planet who is simultaneously the lord of an Angle and Trikona is termed a Yoga Karka. It is capable to endow the native with most things in its period.

Yogini (103)   : One of the Mahadashas. Mostly used in Kashmir and Himachal.

ASTROLOGICAL TERMS

Afflicted (30)* : (*Pirdit*); If a planet or zodiacal sign is teneted, conjoined with or gets an aspect or has a '*Sambandh*' (relationship) with a natural malefic *viz.*, Sun, Mars, Saturn, Rahu or Ketu or with the lords of 6th, 8th, or 12th house then it is termed as afflicted.

Angle (36) : (*Kendra*) : The 1st, 4th, 7th, and 10th house in nativity (horoscope).

Aquarius (4, 6) : (*Kumbha*) : The name of the eleventh sign in the zodiac. Ruled by Saturn (*Shani*); according to the Western Astrologers by Uranus. Fixed (Sthirs). Air (Vayu).

Aries (4, 6) : Mesha. The first sign of the Zodiac. Ruled by Mars; Cardinal (Movable); Fire.

Ascendant (16) : The lagna, or the Rising Sign or the first house in the horoscope. This is calculated according to the date, time and place of birth and is that part of Earth, which is facing towards the Eastern Horizon at birth. Ascendant in fact is also the exact degree on the cusp of the first house.

---

* Numbers given in the brackets after each Astrological terms indicate the page number on which it appears.

Ascending (11)	: Moving upwards and therefore the Zodiac at the birth is called the Ascending sign or Ascendant.
Ascending planets	: Those which are rising eastward towards the Mid-heaven (cusp of 10th house from the 4th house upwards).
Aspects (47)	: 'Drishti'. Planets throw 'drishti' on another planet depending on their placement and in return may also receive Aspect (Drishti) from other planet. The word 'may' is used because in Hindu (Vedic) System of Astrology, Aspects are as follows:

1. All planets aspect the house and planets in the 7th from them.
2. Jupiter in addition also aspects the 5th and 9th houses from its radical position (position at birth in the horoscope).
3. Mars aspects in addition the 4th and 8th houses from itself.
4. Saturn aspects the 3rd and 10th houses.
5. According to some Astrologers, 'Rahu' and 'Ketu' can not have any aspect as they are shadow planets themselves. They show the result of the planets they conjoin with or according to the house and the lord of the sign they are in.

Auspicious (123)	: 'Shubha', Benefic; Natural Benefic are Jupiter, Venus, Moon (Waxing Moon from the 8th lunar day until

the 8ᵗʰ lunar day of the waning Moon) and Mercury, Lords of the 9ᵗʰ, 5ᵗʰ and 1ˢᵗ houses are auspicious.

Benefic (46) : 'Shubha'; Same as above.

Cadent (36) : 'Apoklima'. The term used for the 3ʳᵈ, 6ᵗʰ, 9ᵗʰ, and 12ᵗʰ houses. These are regarded as week houses (except the 9ᵗʰ house). In general Malefics in the 3ʳᵈ and 6ᵗʰ houses show mixed results. They increase the non-living (*viz.*, Valour, Courage, Success over rivals, and are also considered good for jobs) but on the other side, they destroy the living beings and relationship with them *viz.*, Relatives, younger brothers/sisters, maternal relatives etc.

In the 12ᵗʰ house a benefic ensures success in life but Mars, Saturn, Rahu or Ketu create troubles. Sun is good in the 12ᵗʰ house. In Vedic Astrology, all planets in the 9ᵗʰ and 11ᵗʰ houses are deemed to be very good. In Horary Astrology planets in Cadent position cause disappointment and delays.

Cancer (36) : 'Kataka'. The 4ᵗʰ zodiacal sign ruled by Moon; Movable (Chara); Water.

Capricorn (4, 6) : 'Makara'. The 10ᵗʰ sign in the Zodiac, ruled by Saturn; Movable (Chara); Earth.

Caput (7) : Caput Draconis. In Sanskrit, it is called "Rahu". The head of Dragon.

Cauda (7) : Cauda Draconis. In Sanskrit 'Ketu'. The tail of the Dragon. Moon in its orbit around the earth cuts the ecliptic and goes to the North is called the northern (or North) Node of Moon. The corresponding position where the ecliptic is cut and goes to South is the Southern Node of Moon *viz.*, 'Ketu'. Rahu and Ketu always move backwards, They are also called shadow planets or 'Chhaya' Graha. These are considered in Hindu or Vedic Astrology and are powerful.

Combust (53, 85) : 'Asta'. Any planet close to the Sun within $8^{1/2o}$ on either side, is called combust. The opinions differ as to the effects of combustion. Mercury does not get any negative effects. It can travel only within 28° of the Sun. Venus can be within 48° of Sun. These two do not get the negative effect of combustion.

Common (28) : 'Dwisvabhava'; Rashis (Signs). Common signs are Gemini, Virgo, Sagittarius and Pisces. These signs in angles or many planets therein endow one with very acute and intense feelings.

Debilitation (42) : 'Neecha', 'Fall'. When a planet is in a sign opposite to its exaltation sign as Sun in Libra (which is opposite to Aries), it is termed as its sign of debilitation. In the same manner, Moon in Scorpio; Mars in Cancer; Mercury in Pisces; Jupiter in Capricorn; Venus in Virgo; Saturn in Aries. Interpretation is that generally a planet is weak when debilitated.

Directional Strength (51) : Digbala; 'Drikbala'. It is the most important strength of a planet *viz.*, even if a planet is exalted but does not possess directional strength then the resultant effects of the planet will not be very positive, for example: Venus (in Pisces) which is its exaltation sign when placed in the 10th house (where its directional strength is very little) then it will not show its good effects.

Dispositor (83) : Rashish *i.e.*, the lord of the sign occupied by a planet is called its dispositor.

Ecliptic (3) : The circle which the Sun appears to describe. The name comes from the fact that Eclipses are termed in this area.

Evil Houses (36, 83) : The 6th, 8th, and 12th houses are called Evil houses.

Exaltation (42) : 'Uchcha'; (Higher state of being). A powerful dignity. Many planets in their exaltation bring the native to prominence in life. The native rises far above his sphere of birth. Three exalted planets makes one a Minister to a King. Four planets or more a *Sanyasi* (an Ascetic) or a King.

Gemini (4, 6) : 'Mithuna'. The third sign of the Zodiac. Ruled by Mercury; Mutable (Dwiswabhava); Air (Vayu).

House (17) : 'Bhava'. The twelfth part of the Zodiac not necessarily of equal portions. There are two types of houses. The house of the planets is of which they are the rulers. The other houses are the Mundane houses *viz.*, the 1st, 2nd, 3rd, etc. in the chart.

Inauspicious (121) : 'Ashubh'; (not benefic, 'papa').

Leo—Simha (4, 6)	:	The fifth sign of the zodiac ruled by Sun; Fixed (Sthir); Fire (Agni).
Libra—Tula (4, 6)	:	The seventh sign of the zodiac ruled by Venus; Cardinal (Movable); Air (Vayu).
Lord of (27, 85)	:	'Rashish'; Ruler of the sign.
Malefic (46)	:	'Papa'; Sun, Mars, Saturn, Rahu and Ketu are malefics.
Moon Sign (87)	:	Rashi. The sign occupied by Moon (Chandra) at birth.
Nodes (7)	:	Rahu and Ketu are called the Nodes (of Moon).
Owner of (35)	:	Rahish. The ruler of the sign.
Periods (103)	:	Dashas. These are calculated according to the degree (longitude) of Moon at birth. The balance of mahadasha (called 'Bhogya') at birth will come. The period elapsed before birth (called 'Bhukta') can be known by deducing the balance from the total duration of the mahadasha of the planet allotted to it. For example, the total duration of Sun in the Vimshottari Dasha System is six years. When the longitude of Moon in Virgo is seven degrees, the balance of the period of Sun is 1 year, 4 months and 6 days. The bhukta dasha is (Total duration—the balance) which in this example gives us 4 years, 7 months and 24 days.

The Mahadashas of the nine planets from Sun, Moon Mars, Rahu etc. are in cyclic order. These are further divided into Antardashas and then further into Pratyantardashas.

Pisces (4, 6) : Meena; the 12th sign in the zodiac. Ruled by Jupiter Dwisvabhava (mutable); Water.

Precession (5) : Calculation of a horoscope in the Western Astrology is done for the Tropical Zodiac; '0' degree *i.e.,* the commencing point in the Tropical zodiac is ever moving backwards (preceding) at the rate of 52" per year (app.). The distance between the commencing points in the Tropical and the Sidreal Zodiacs was 23 degrees, 29 minutes and 4 seconds on 1st January, 1973. This difference between the commencing points in the two systems is called the precession or the precession of the equinoxes. Please note that the Zodiac is only one but it is the difference in the point of commencement that gives us the two systems.

"There is a motion of the earth upon its axis somewhat like that of a boy's top, which, set spinning with its axis inclined to the vertical, moves so that the axis slowly describes a vertical cone. The Earth's axis gyrates in a cone while keeping its inclination to the ecliptic practically unchanged, however the gyration is so slow that the complete circuit takes about 25,800 years. This motion of the earth is called Precession." (Quote from John Charles Duncan's *Astronomy*).

Radical (107) : 'Janmakalik'. The position of planets etc. pertaining to the radix of natal chart.

Radix (107)   : The birth chart or the natal chart.

Right Ascension (15)   : The distance of a planet from the
                             first point of Aries measuring along
                             the equator is called the right
                             Ascension.

RAMC (15)   : Right Ascension of the Meridian
                             Cusp. It is the sidereal time at birth.
                             The Ascendant and cusps of houses
                             are calculated on the basis of
                             RAMC.

Relationship   : Two types of relationship: (1) Tem-
(42, 43, 44, 45)   porary and (2) Permanent. Please
                             see pages 42 to 45.

Retrograde (19)   : 'Vakri'. Apparent backward motion of
                             planet. No planet moves backwards,
                             only its relative forward motion is
                             slower and so it looks as if it is
                             moving backwards or receding. In
                             Hindu Astrology, a malefic when
                             retrograde becomes more evil but
                             on the other hand, a benefic in
                             retrograde motion becomes more
                             positive. When a planet is stationary
                             then it is at its meridian to show
                             effect. At times when Jupiter is
                             stationary then the father dies but
                             inheritance is received. So the
                             planets show effect in diverse
                             manners. Stationary Jupiter (at birth)
                             was found in the horoscopes of
                             people from wealthy families.

Rising (7)   : Udaya. (See Ascending).

Ruler (35)   : Swami; lord of *viz.,* Moon is the
                             ruler of Cancer; Sun is the ruler of
                             Leo etc. If a sign falls in a house
                             viz., Leo in the fifth house then we
                             say that the Sun is the ruler of the
                             5th house.

Sagittarius (4, 6)	: Dhanu; the ninth house in the Zodiac; Dwiswabhava (mutable); Fire.
Scorpio (4, 6)	: Vrischik; the eight sign of the Zodiac; Sthira (Fixed); Water.
Sidereal (4, 6)	: It is the (fixed) star time. Sidereal or Nirayan chart is used in Hindu system as compared to the Tropical or Sayan system in Western Astrology.
Significator (88)	: Karaka. Each planet has a connection with certain matters or persons *viz.*, Sun signifies father, Atma, (Soul), Dignity, etc. Moon signifies mother, emotional system, wealth, popularity etc. When the significator for a planet is strong then good results follow in the matters and subjects signified by the planet and vice versa. If the native however does not have a good relationship with a living person signified by a planet then that planet will never be able to show any remarkable results even if it has all the strength in the chart. On the other hand, a debilitated and weak planet exerts beautiful and positive results when the person signified by it, has a good relationship with the native. For example, Mars stands for brothers/sisters and you can get positive results when you please your brothers and sisters; keep the wife happy and the Moon and Venus will show good results for all matters which fall under

them. If we do not understand the importance of the 'Karak' then the interpretations of a chart can baffle us.

Signs (27, 28, 29)   : Rashi. Division of the Zodiacs into twelve signs of thirty degrees each. These signs are called Aries, Taurus, Gemini, etc.

Subdivisions (30)   : When a sign of 30 degree is divided further than these are called subdivisions. In the Hindu system, a sign is divided into 2, 3, 6, 7, 9, 10 portions etc. In order to assess the strength of a planet by its placement in various subdivision. Out of this Navansha (9th part), which consists of 3 degrees and 20 minutes each, is the most important. A planet strong in Navansha by virtue of being in its own sign, exaltation etc., improves the horoscope. This is in fact the heart of the horoscope. The judgment of spouse is done from the Navansha chart.

Sub periods (103)   : Antardashas; Antar. Please see periods above.

Succedent (36)   : Panaphara. The houses which succeed the Angles *viz.*, 2nd, 5th, 8th, and 11th.

Taurus (4, 6)   : Vrishabha. The second sign of the Zodiac; Fixed; Earth.

Temporary (65)   : 'Tatkalik'. Temporary friendship between planets depending upon their placement in a chart. If a planet is in the 2nd, 3rd, 4th, 10th, 11th, and 12th, from a planet, it is a temporary friend and the other planets will be enemies.

Transit (135) : 'Gochara'. The movements of planets through different signs of the zodiac. It is very important for the timing of the events. The transit of a planet becomes very significant when a planet or planets are posited in a sign through which it is passing or throwing an aspect.. It is special when in the sign occupied by the Moon or the signs preceding and succeeding the Janmarashi.

Trine (36) : 'Trikona'. The 5th, and the 9th houses are called Trine. The 1st house is an angle and a trine both.

Tropical (4) : 'Sayan'; Ayanvritam'. Cancer and Capricorn are also referred to as tropical (signs).

Virgo (4, 6) : 'Kanya'. The sixth sign in the zodiac. Mutable (Dwiswabhava); Earth.

Zodiac (4) : Jyotishchakram or Mandalam. There are two of them Celestial *i.e.*, one is the Zodiac of the Constellation; the other is the Mathematical Zodiac used by Astronomers and Astrologers.